It's About Time

It's About TIME

How Long History Took

Mike Flanagan

**Andrews McMeel
Publishing**

Kansas City

04 05 06 07 08 MLT 10 9 8 7 6 5 4 3 2 1

Library of Congress Cataloging-in-Publication Data

Flanagan, Mike
   It's about time : how long history took / Mike Flanagan.
      p. cm.
   ISBN: 0-7407-4694-4
   1. United States—History—Anecdotes. 2. World history—Anecdotes. 3. Time—History—Anecdotes. I. Title.

E178.6.F55 2004
973—dc22

                                                          2004056044

Book design by Pete Lippincott

For
Nancy

"Time flies over us, but leaves its shadow behind."

—NATHANIEL HAWTHORNE
The Marble Faun

Introduction

TIME HAS BEEN WITH US from the beginning, invisible, untouchable, and ever present. Early people were aware of it, watching the stars gradually change their positions, experiencing the shifts of seasons, measuring their days, knowing when it was time to eat and time to sleep.

As civilizations evolved, so too did our concepts of time. The scientists believed time resided in the heavens, as sure as destiny and astrology. The mathematicians were sure it was their arena, filled with numbers and calculations. The historians knew that they were the true owners of time; how else could they record achievements as well as conflicts? And the philosophers, not to be forgotten, maintained that wisdom and experience were the true manifestations of time. The fact that we started as helpless babies, blossomed into functional adults, and then progressed into decrepitude was a cosmic message for the only animal that demanded the meaning of life.

For this book, we'll go along with the historian. It's about time as it relates to the durations of historical incidents, great and small. Time is a big part of history, but it often gets lost in the excitement. We have not always been able to witness history as it happens. Now that we can, we can still be fooled by time.

This collection began as a newspaper article in 1986 shortly after the *Challenger* disaster. Over and over, television networks kept running the all-too-quick video of the complete mission of NASA's doomed space shuttle. Start to finish, 73 seconds. Lives ended, lives changed, our collective thoughts about the commonplace safety of modern space travel got rearranged in just over a minute.

At the time, as news anchors came to grips with the tragedy and stayed on camera far into the night, they began to reflect on the JFK assassination in 1963, and how unique, personal memories would be attached to this event as well. They also talked of Pearl Harbor—how history can jolt us to our very core. All this was echoed again September 11, 2001.

Working on a premise of time, I sought out the durations of a handful of other historic events, including the sinking of the *Titanic,* Custer's trip to the Little Bighorn, and Neil Armstrong's stroll on the moon. It was fascinating putting it all together; I was often surprised by the results.

History begins in the form of news. News comes to us two ways: planned, as in a press conference or a scheduled event, and more often than not, by complete surprise. However it develops, there is always a time frame, a beginning and end. Whether it is a surprise attack, the creation of a work of art, or a conflict that took so long it was called the Hundred Years' War, the element of time is always there. Even if the event might be too complex to grasp in total, we can at least identify with the impact of time.

Timing history is another matter. In the preelectronic era, a lot of the chronicling was logged in by experts who weren't there. As true reporting came of age, times of day and durations become part of the stories.

How time has been calculated over the years could be a book of its own. Showing the passage of time on common calendars has always been a problem because the interval between successive vernal equinoxes is 365.2424 days. To adjust for what works out to 11 minutes less than 365 and a quarter days, the ancient Egyptians broke it down into 24-hour days, a dozen 30-day months, then added five days at the end of the year.

The Mesopotamians came up with hours and seconds, and from the Near East we got seven-day weeks. Julius Caesar decided the calendar should be based on the movement of the sun and created "leap years" every fourth year with 366 days. One year he also had to add two months between November and December to get the vernal equinox back to the 25th of March, and he never bothered to beware the Ides of March. But that's a different story.

In turn, he gave the odd months (first, third, fifth, seventh, ninth) 31 days and the rest 30, except for February. That was assigned 29 days in a regular year and 30 in a leap year. When Augustus came into power, he couldn't allow his month to have fewer days than Julius's (July), so he cut a day from February and pasted it into August. Further balance trimmed September and November down to 30 days and set October and December at 31.

Things seemed fine for a while. It didn't seem to be a huge deal that the vernal equinox was lagging back one day every 130 years. By 1500, however, spring was busting out around March 10 and autumn was falling around September 13, both a little on the early side. Throwing the farmers off was one thing, but messing with Easter, which should have been taking place around Passover on the lunar Jewish calendar, was a major no-no. Jesuit mathematician Christoph Clavius got the call from Pope Gregory to fix it as soon as possible.

In 1582, things changed. The pope ordered 10 days to be dropped from October that year, which put the vernal equinox back to March 20. To fix that business of an extra day every 130 years, papal decree scratched three leap years every 400 years. This is why 1700, 1800, and 1900 were not leap years, but 1600 and 2000 were.

Working the math was one thing; getting people to accept it all was something else. Rome adopted the Gregorian calendar immediately. Germany and the Netherlands came on board within a few decades. The British, and in turn her American colonies, refused to change calendars for two and a half centuries. When the change was finally adopted, George Washington found his birthday had jumped from February 11 to February 22.

And of course other cultures around the globe such as the Aztecs, Mayas, Incas, and Chinese were measuring time by their own calendars.

For the purposes of this book, a minute is 60 seconds, an hour is 60 minutes, a day is 24 hours, and a week is seven days. One month is a calendar month, whether it took 28 or 31 days. And, a year is a year, whether it took 365 or 366 days. Now, if the incident (like the final battle of the Alamo) took place over a leap day, then, of course, that day is included.

When it is in progress, history is a current event coming to us in pieces of lightning called bulletins. Breaking news has been important to all generations, but we have progressed to a point where our electronic capabilities bring us history in real time.

The timing of history is fascinating as well as important. It adds to our understanding of particular events to know not only how long they took, but also what time of day they happened and even what day it was. Imagine not knowing that the attack on Pearl Harbor happened on a Sunday morning.

Monumental proceedings can happen in less than a minute, yet create a century of memories, while things that take thousands of years to evolve are more often than not relegated to a sentence or two in a forgotten textbook.

To keep entries as accurate as possible, I have used the GEDCOM date calendar developed by Professor John A. Nairn of the University of Utah Material Science and Engineering Department. This calendar was developed for genealogy calculations and supports the Gregorian, Julian, Hebrew, and French Republic calendars.

Despite advances in technology, we are still dealing with humans who kept time, so there is always room for an error. Not everyone is as precise as NASA, who times every event down to the millisecond. The guys who pulled off the St. Valentine's Day Massacre, for instance, didn't leave any timely evidence behind, so we are forced to rely on newspaper accounts. Sources have been checked and rechecked, giving you the most accurate times available. Should accounts change over time, the times will be corrected in future editions.

Where possible, times of day have been included. We can't say for sure the start time of the last ice age, but we do know that Charles Lindbergh took off on his flight across the Atlantic at 7:52 a.m. on May 20, 1927. Rather than attempting to standardize with Greenwich Mean or military time, times of day are local to the time zone in which they occurred, unless otherwise noted. Also, as time lengths increase, so do individual interpretations. For the really long durations, we are in the realm of approximation based on the best current knowledge.

Unlike most history books that present events in chronological order, here they are ranked by time, shortest to longest. We start with an incident that took a fraction of a second and end with one that is still unfolding, 14 billion years and counting. In between are selected events, when they occurred, and how long they took—brief glimpses of the past when it was the present.

It's about a lot of things, but mostly, it's about time.

Photographing the Flag Raising on Iwo Jima

Wartime photographer Joe Rosenthal captures one of the most memorable images of World War II.

TIME FELT suspended on the island of Iwo Jima after 72 consecutive days of naval bombardment. Now the Fifth Marines Division had landed to finish the job, flushing out the remaining Japanese defenders from a network of catacombs. On the fourth day of the operation, February 23, 1945, Col. Chandler Johnson called for a large flag to be planted on Mount Suribachi, a dormant volcano. Associated Press photographer Joe Rosenthal perched on a pile of sandbags, set his shutter for 1/400th of a second, and snapped the most famous picture of World War II as Rene Gagnon, John Bradley, Mike Strank, Harlan Block, Frank Sousley, and Ira Hayes hoisted a 20-foot pipe that bore the American flag.

Bobby Thomson's
Shot Heard Round the World

Bobby Thomson is mobbed by his teammates at home plate.

"BASEBALL'S GREATEST MOMENT" came on October 3, 1951, at New York's Polo Grounds. In just over seven weeks, the New York Giants had closed in on the Brooklyn Dodgers 13-game lead to finish tied for first at season's end. In the third and deciding playoff game, Brooklyn was up 4–2 in the bottom of the ninth when Bobby Thomson came to bat with two men on base and sent Ralph Branca's second pitch into the left field stands. Radio listeners heard the crack of Thomson's bat followed almost immediately by commentator Russ Hodge's first bursts of "The Giants win the pennant! The Giants win the pennant!"

The Assassination of President Kennedy

The route of the JFK motorcade on a souvenir postcard.

COMMENTING ON THE NICE WEATHER, President John F. Kennedy requested that the protective bubble top be removed from the Lincoln Continental in which he would be riding through Dallas, Texas, on November 22, 1963. His motorcade departed Love Field at 11:55 a.m. Shots rang out at 12:30 as his car passed slowly through crowded Dealy Plaza. He was admitted to Parkland Memorial Hospital at 12:38. Walter Cronkite delivered the first televised bulletin at 12:40. By 1:00 p.m., when JFK was officially pronounced dead, 75 million Americans knew about the shooting. In 1964, the Warren Commission findings set the time of the three shots at 5.6 seconds, based on silent amateur film shot by Abraham Zapruder. In 1979, an acoustical analysis in the Report of the Select Committee on Assassinations of the U.S. House of Representatives maintained that 8.3 seconds elapsed between the first and final shots.

The First Flight of the Wright Brothers

Wilbur Wright watches brother Orville make the first flight at Kitty Hawk, North Carolina.

THEY HAD WORKED as printers and bicycle manufacturers, but brothers Orville and Wilbur Wright found themselves captivated by the aeronautical experiments of Otto Lilienthal. Their tests and experiments became serious in 1901 when they constructed a wind tunnel to test such far-flung ideas as wind resistance. On December 17, 1903, they successfully tested the first heavier-than-air machine (745 pounds) at Kitty Hawk, North Carolina, with Orville flying at an altitude of ten feet and a distance of 120 feet. Three flights followed that day. On the last one, Wilbur flew 852 feet in 57 seconds.

The Long Count

Scene of "The Long Count," Soldier Field, 1927. The referee wouldn't start the count until Jack Dempsey moved to an opposite corner.

GENE TUNNEY WON a decision over Jack Dempsey in 1926, setting up the rematch of the century. On September 22, 1927, 104,943 people paid $2,658,660 to see the main event at Chicago's Soldier Field. In the first 50 seconds of the seventh round, Dempsey's lethal left hook sent Tunney to the mat. Referee Dave Barry wouldn't begin the count until Dempsey moved to a neutral corner. By the time Dempsey relocated, precious seconds—at least 14, perhaps as many as 18—had ticked away. Tunney stood up at the count of nine and went on to win another decision. Appeals to the state boxing commission and the National Boxing Association were rejected and "The Long Count" went into history as one of boxing's greatest controversies.

Jesse Owens's Olympic Record

Undefeated in 42 track events for Ohio State that year, Jesse Owens brought it on at the 1936 Berlin Olympics.

ADOLF HITLER's dreams of an Aryan sweep at the Berlin Olympics were dashed by an African American athlete with dreams of his own. First, Ohio State track star Jesse Owens, 22, won the 100-meter (10.3 seconds) and the long jump. Then, on August 5, 1936, he completed his quest for triple gold with a record-setting 200-meter run of 20.7 seconds. On August 9, he won his fourth gold, leading the 4 × 100-meter U.S. relay team to another world record of 39.8 seconds.

The Gunfight at the O.K. Corral

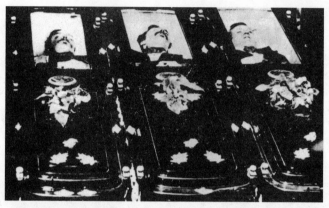

Even the *Tombstone Epitaph* took note of the suddenness: "Three Men Hurled into Eternity in the Duration of a Moment." Frank McLaury, Tom McLaury, and Billy Clanton, on their way to Boothill.

A BITTER RIVALRY erupted into violence in Tombstone, Arizona, on the afternoon of October 26, 1881. Wyatt Earp, along with his lawmen brothers Virgil and Morgan and their dentist friend Doc Holliday, had been spoiling for a fight with rancher Ike Clanton. Hearing that the Earps were gunning for them, Ike, his son, and two hired hands decided to avoid a confrontation. Hoping to ride out of town, they headed for their horses at the Old West's most famous livery stable. The Earps and Doc Holliday met them there, and after a quick verbal exchange, opened fire. Ike Clanton ran, but his son Billy Clanton and brothers Frank and Tom McLaury were slain. Witnesses claim to have heard 25 or 30 shots.

The *Hindenburg* Disaster

Because an act of Congress prevented the United States from selling helium to Nazi Germany, the *Hindenburg* was filled with highly flammable hydrogen.

THE $5 MILLION, 804-FOOT-LONG Nazi luxury zeppelin had just flown across the Atlantic from Frankfurt, Germany, and was preparing to land on May 6, 1937, at Lakehurst, New Jersey. The first spark was seen at 7:23 p.m. near the tail fin as the airship hovered about 200 feet above the ground. Herb Morrison of Chicago's WLS radio delivered his historic eyewitness account as the dirigible was engulfed in flame and 35 lives were lost.

The St. Valentine's Day Massacre

When informed of the slaughter on Clark Street, Bugs Moran said, "Only Capone kills like that."

SHORTLY AFTER 10:00 a.m. on February 14, 1929, what appeared to be a routine liquor bust turned into a bloodbath. Seven members of Bugs Moran's gang were lined up against a wall in a Chicago warehouse and executed by four men posing as police. Authorities found over a hundred spent shells from machine guns capable of firing 1,500 rounds a minute. The assailants, believed to be working on orders from Al Capone, departed immediately. The crime was never officially solved.

Dropping the First Atomic Bomb

Hiroshima aftermath, where the temperature had reached 7,000 degrees.

THE MISSION TO HIROSHIMA began with the *Enola Gay* taking off at 2:45 a.m. from Tinian Island in the Marianas on August 6, 1945. At 8:15:17 a.m. (Hiroshima time), "Little Boy," the first atom bomb to be used in wartime, dropped from the B-29 bomber. At 8:16 it detonated 1,900 feet above the courtyard of Shima Hospital with a yield equivalent to 12,500 tons of TNT. Approximately 80,000 Japanese and 23 American POWs were dead within the first hour. Radiation-related illnesses would eventually claim another 130,000 lives. The *Enola Gay* returned to Tinian at 2:58 p.m., 12 hours, 13 minutes after takeoff.

The Oklahoma City Bombing

Ruins of the Murrah Building, Oklahoma City, 1995.

ON APRIL 19, 1995, Timothy McVeigh ignited a fuse to a 2-ton fuel oil and fertilizer bomb he had packed inside a rented Ryder truck and parked in front of the north face of the nine-story Alfred P. Murrah Federal Building. The 9:02 a.m. blast, at the time the deadliest terrorist attack ever carried out on U.S. soil, killed 167 people, including 19 children who were in a second-floor day care center.

Edward VIII's Abdication Speech

After the storm, the Duke and Duchess of Windsor in 1940.

KING EDWARD VIII, 42, resigned the British throne in a 10:00 p.m. radio address delivered from Windsor Castle on December 11, 1936. King for only 325 days since the death of his father, King George V, Edward's desire to marry American divorcée Wallis Warfield Simpson had caused a royal uproar. In the end, he chose to vacate his throne.

The Flight of the *Challenger*

Five seconds after the *Challenger* explodes, disbelief is about to set in.

THE SPACE SHUTTLE *Challenger,* carrying a crew of seven including teacher Christa McAuliffe, was launched just after 11:38 a.m. on Tuesday, January 28, 1986. Suddenly, a violent chain reaction unfolded before huge live and television audiences. A large puff of smoke from the solid rocket booster appeared at launch plus .678 seconds followed by a burning plume at 58.7888 seconds. Structural failures in the liquid hydrogen and liquid oxygen tanks occurred at 73.124 and 73.137 seconds. The "total vehicle breakup" happened at 73.213 seconds, as the shuttle was traveling at an altitude of 46,000 feet at speeds of nearly 2,000 mph.

The San Francisco Earthquake

Stunned residents watch helplessly as their city crumbles.

THE DISASTROUS EVENTS OF APRIL 18, 1906, began with a tremor at 5:13 in the morning. The ground undulated and broke, buildings toppled, and San Francisco rudely awakened to a tragedy of major proportions. Subsequent fires, aided by the wind and broken water mains, consumed 3,000 acres, including 28,188 buildings. Over 700 people were killed in the calamity that stretched over a three-day period.

The Gettysburg Address

The only known photograph from the dedication ceremonies. Lincoln is just a face in the crowd.

ON NOVEMBER 2, 1863, David Wills invited President Abraham Lincoln to make a "few appropriate remarks" at the consecration of the Soldiers National Cemetery where the battle of Gettysburg had been fought the previous July. Rhetorician Edward Everett was also invited, and spoke for two hours at the November 19 ceremony. Around 3:00 p.m., Lincoln rose and delivered the speech of his life in 272 words.

The First Four-Minute Mile

Roger Bannister broke his record of May 6 on August 9 with a time of 3:58.8. It is believed some 2,000 runners have broken the four-minute mile since then, with the record of 3:43.13 set by Hicham El Guerrouj of Morocco in 1999.

THE FIRST RUNNER to break the barrier of four minutes for one mile was Roger Bannister, 25, before a crowd of 3,000 at Oxford University on May 6, 1954. He completed the first lap in 57.5 seconds, and reached the half-mile mark at 1:58. Realizing he had 59 seconds to complete the last lap, Bannister recalled, "Those last few seconds seemed never-ending. . . . The arms of the world were waiting to receive me if only I reached the tape without slackening my speed. If I faltered, there would be no arms to hold me and the world would be a cold, forbidding place, because I had been so close."

The Beatles on *Ed Sullivan*

Ed Sullivan gets a backstage guitar lesson from the Fab Four, as Brian Epstein looks on.

THE BRITISH INVASION reached a fever pitch with the first appearance of the Beatles on *The Ed Sullivan Show* the evening of February 9, 1964. John Lennon, Paul McCartney, George Harrison, and Ringo Starr played two segments as 73 million Americans tuned in. In this, their first set, they played "All My Loving," "'Til There Was You," and "She Loves You." Later in the show they played another 5 minutes and 40 seconds. This was the first of four performances by the group on the Sullivan show, the final of which occurred September 12, 1965.

Richard Nixon's "Checkers Speech"

Every dog has his day. The vice-presidential candidate and Checkers.

DWIGHT D. EISENHOWER'S VICE-PRESIDENTIAL CANDIDATE answered charges of campaign fund misuse in a televised address on September 23, 1952. During the speech, Nixon laid out his financial history with folksy candor, acknowledging that there was one thing he did accept—a puppy that a supporter had sent his young daughters. The speech was met with enthusiasm as Nixon spun a public relations nightmare into a campaigning miracle.

Richard Nixon's Resignation Speech

President Nixon addressed the nation on the evening of August 8, 1974. Everyone watching knew what he would say, but it hardly lessened the impact.

THE WATERGATE SCANDAL ended with the first presidential resignation in American history. When the events of over two years began to unravel into the threat of an impeachment, the end was near. In a televised address from the White House at 9:00 p.m. on August 8, 1974, Richard Milhous Nixon, 61, the 37th president, announced his decision to resign. It was his 2,027th day in office. In his address, he announced he would leave office at noon the next day. Vice President Gerald R. Ford would finish out the 895 days remaining in Nixon's term.

First U.S. Manned Space Flight

Alan Shepard missed being the first man in space by 23 days, but one day he would hit a golf ball on the moon.

U.S. NAVY COMMANDER Alan B. Shepard Jr., 37, was launched from Cape Canaveral, Florida, on a suborbital flight at 9:34 a.m., May 5, 1961. His Mercury *Freedom* 7 capsule went 116 miles into space, reaching speeds of 5,134 mph. It landed 303 miles out at sea and was lifted out of the waters by a Marine Corps helicopter. In 1971, Shepard became the fifth man to walk on the moon.

Martin Luther King Jr.'s "I Have a Dream" Speech

Martin Luther King Jr. embraces history on a hot afternoon in Washington, D.C.

ONE HUNDRED YEARS and 24 days after the Emancipation Proclamation, 250,000 people gathered at the Lincoln Memorial for "a march on Washington for jobs and freedom." The Reverend Dr. Martin Luther King Jr., 34, the last speaker of the day, took the podium around 5:00 p.m. President Kennedy, watching a White House television, was impressed how King left his prepared text and spoke from his heart. Greeting King in the Cabinet Room at the end of the day, Kennedy smiled and said, "I have a dream." In 2002, a survey of 137 speech and communications professors ranked King's speech as the greatest political speech of the 20th century.

The Sinking of the *Lusitania*

Three years after the *Titanic*, a purposely sunk passenger liner puts the United States on the path to war.

ON MAY 1, 1915, the British Cunard Line steamship *Lusitania* sailed from America for Liverpool with 1,257 passengers (including young millionaire Alfred Vanderbilt) and a crew of 702. A wartime warning published by Germany in New York newspapers reminded passengers of the dangers of sea travel. At 2:10 p.m. on May 7, 14 miles from Kinsale, Ireland, a torpedo from the German submarine U-20 hit the ship. It sank at 2:28 p.m. The incident claimed 1,198 lives, 128 of them American, and became a major factor in leading the United States into intervention in World War I. Today the *Lusitania* lies on its starboard side in 295 feet of water.

Edward White's Walk in Space

James McDivitt aimed his camera out the hatch to capture Ed White's
historic spacewalk.

MAJ. EDWARD H. WHITE II, 34, stepped out of his *Gemini IV* capsule
during its third orbit 135 miles over Hawaii, 4 hours and 30 minutes
into the flight, at 2:45 p.m., June 3, 1965. It was the first Extra Vehicular
Activity (EVA) for NASA and only the second time a space traveler had
left his ship. His 17,500 mph spacewalk concluded when ground control
notified him it was time to rejoin his fellow astronaut, Commander
James McDivitt. Just before White reentered, he looked over his shoulder
at the earth below and saw Florida.

The First Untethered Manned Balloon Flight

An artist's conception of the big day in Paris, when men flew.

JOSEPH-MICHEL MONTGOLFIER loved to watch the clouds drifting by. One night while observing smoke rising from his fire, he fashioned a small silk pouch and found that it too could rise when filled with heated air. One experiment led to another until June 14, 1783, when he and his brother Jacques-Etienne flew a 38-foot linen bag a distance of one mile. At Versailles on September 19, Louis XVI looked on as a sheep, a duck, and a rooster ascended into the clouds and returned safely. On November 21, 1783, physicist Jean-François Pilâtre de Rozier and François Laurent, Marquis d'Arlandes, became the first men to fly without a tether. They went up almost 3,000 feet, flew almost six miles, and landed on the outskirts of Paris. The event was witnessed by a crowd of 400,000.

Custer's Last Stand

Confident to the point of foolhardiness, Custer the conqueror.

NEARING THE LITTLE BIGHORN RIVER, Lt. Col. George Armstrong Custer, 36, split his Seventh Cavalry command into three battalions at 12:07 P.M. on the hot afternoon of June 25, 1876. He sent Maj. Reno to attack the Indian encampment from the south, and told Capt. Benteen to move toward the southwest and engage where he could. Custer then proceeded with five companies, some 215 men, to attack from the front. What he ran into was perhaps the largest such gathering ever on the continent— 10,000 Indians, including 2,000 warriors. Sitting Bull made medicine in his tent while Crazy Horse and Gall led the counterattack. Custer and all of his men were wiped out. One Cheyenne estimated the battle lasted "as long as it took the sun to travel the width of a lodge pole."

The War of the Worlds Broadcast

New York World-Telegram

U. S. Investigates Radio Drama of Invasion By Martians That Threw Nation Into Panic

Scare Analyzed By Psychologists

H. G. Wells Indignant Over Liberties Taken With His Book

They Say Panic Sho Lack of Imagination

Welles on Wells, an open-armed apology on Halloween morning.

INSPIRED BY HERB MORRISON's *Hindenburg* broadcast, Orson Welles, 23, led his Mercury Players in a Halloween eve radio production of H. G. Wells's *The War of the Worlds* that had a bit of a twist. The show would be broadcast as if it were really happening, complete with news bulletins. An opening disclaimer aired at 8:00 p.m. the evening of October 30, 1938, but it is believed many listeners missed it because they were tuned to Edgar Bergen and Charlie McCarthy on another network. Eventually, an audience of 6 million tuned in, 1.2 million who actually believed Mars attacked.

The Attack on Pearl Harbor

The magazine of the USS *Shaw* explodes while being bombed by Japanese aircraft at 9:30 a.m. during the attack on Pearl Harbor on December 7, 1941.

THE REASON FOR THE SURPRISE ATTACK was simple—knock out the U.S. Pacific fleet and hope to gain quick superiority in the coming war. Most of the fleet was docked at Pearl Harbor on the island of Oahu, Hawaii— some 75 battleships, cruisers, destroyers, and submarines. Admiral Nagumo's 366 carrier-based Japanese bombers, fighters, and torpedo planes began the bombardment at 7:55 a.m., December 7, 1941. The first wave lasted approximately 52 minutes. Around 9:00 a.m., 168 additional aircraft swarmed in for another round of death and destruction. By 9:35 a.m., 19 ships had been sunk or severely damaged, 188 aircraft had been destroyed, and 159 damaged. A total of 2,403 soldiers and sailors as well as 107 civilians were dead.

Terrorist Attacks of 9/11

Stunned onlookers witnessed the final moments of the World Trade Center.

ALTHOUGH THE AIRLINERS WERE HIJACKED earlier in the morning, the tragic events began to unfold with the crash of American Airlines Flight 11 into floors 79 through 95 of the north tower of the World Trade Center at 8:46:26 a.m. on September 11, 2001. Then United Flight 175 hit the south tower at 9:02:54 a.m. While confusion reigned in New York City, American Airlines Flight 77 plunged into the Pentagon at 9:38 a.m. At 9:59:04 a.m., just 57 minutes after impact, the south tower of the World Trade Center crumbled. Shortly after, passengers on United Airlines Flight 93 overwhelmed their hijackers, sending the airplane into a field 80 miles southeast of Pittsburgh at 10:03:11 a.m. At 10:28:31 a.m. the World Trade Center's north tower came down. At press time, the latest statistics had 2,749 people losing their lives at the World Trade Center, 184 at the Pentagon, and 40 near Shanksville, Pennsylvania.

The First Manned Space Flight

Yuri Gagarin was back on the ground before the Soviets announced their achievement.

FOR RUSSIAN COSMONAUT YURI GAGARIN, 27, it was either to be a day of heroism or the day he died—one or the other. At 9:07 a.m. on Wednesday, April 12, 1961, his five-ton *Vostok 1* capsule was fired into space by an R-7 rocket from Baikonur. Gagarin carried a small doll with him; when it floated he knew he had reached zero gravity. He completed one orbit, reaching an altitude of 187 miles. Although the flight was automated, Gagarin had an emergency key to unlock the controls in the event he would be required to fly the craft. The young pilot ejected 108 minutes into the mission and parachuted safely, landing near the remote village of Smelovka near Engels. The capsule drifted to earth on its parachutes ten minutes later.

The Midnight Ride of Paul Revere

Revere awakens the countryside on his historic ride.

REVERE, A COURIER for the Massachusetts Committee of Safety, recorded his wildest night on April 18, 1775. Dr. Joseph Warren dispatched him to Lexington, Massachusetts, to warn John Hancock and Samuel Adams of approaching British troops. Revere rowed to Charlestown, saw two lanterns shining from Boston's Old North Church, the signal that the redcoats would invade by sea, and took off on horseback about 11:00 p.m. After spreading the word along the way, he found Hancock and Adams in Lexington at midnight. With William Dawes and Dr. Samuel Prescott, he rode toward Concord. The British surprised them at 1:00 a.m. and Paul was finished riding for the evening. Dawes and Prescott escaped, but Revere was held until 2:00 a.m. His horse confiscated, he walked back to Lexington.

Neil Armstrong's Walk on the Moon

Armstrong and Aldrin erect their specially frame-fitted flag designed to "fly" on a surface with no atmosphere.

IT WAS SUNDAY, JULY 20, 1969, and much of the world was watching a live telecast from the moon, courtesy of NASA's *Apollo XI* mission. Following a 4:18 p.m. eastern daylight time (EDT) landing at the Sea of Tranquility and a six-hour wait inside the lunar module *Eagle,* Neil Armstrong took his "one small step for man" at 10:56:15 p.m. Edwin "Buzz" Aldrin joined him on the lunar surface at 11:15:15 p.m. for an outing that was seen by 600 million people. The pair conducted experiments and collected 47 pounds of rocks from the lunar surface. The *Eagle* stayed on the moon for 21 hours, 36 minutes; *Apollo XI*'s mission lasted eight days, three hours, and 18 minutes.

2 hours, **40** minutes • **1912**

The Sinking of the *Titanic*

Artist's conception of the night the great ship went down.

THE RMS *TITANIC* SAILED ON HER MAIDEN VOYAGE from Southampton on April 10, 1912. She was the "unsinkable" pride of the White Star Line, with 2,228 people on board. At 11:39 on the night of April 14, the ship was cruising at 20.5 knots when lookouts Fredrick Fleet and Reginald Lee spotted an iceberg towering 60 feet above the water less than 500 yards away. From the sighting through the collision that hit the starboard bow side, just 37 seconds passed. Many passengers didn't even feel it. Within 10 minutes, water had risen 14 feet inside the doomed ship. The last lifeboat left at 2:05 a.m., leaving 1,500 people on board. At 2:20 a.m. on April 15, the 46,428-ton luxury liner slipped beneath the icy waves.

The Boston Tea Party

The colonists were restless that night.

ON THE NIGHT OF DECEMBER 16, 1773, Samuel Adams led 150 Sons of Liberty in a unique protest. Upset with the tea tax levied by Great Britain, they painted their faces, dressed like Mohawk Indians, and boarded three docked ships, the *Dartmouth*, the *Beaver*, and the *Eleanor*. They used axes and hammers to crack 342 chests of tea, then threw the contents overboard into Boston harbor. The tea was valued at £9,000.

John Glenn's Flight

John Glenn climbs aboard his *Friendship* 7 capsule, February 20, 1962.

ON FEBRUARY 20, 1962, Marine Corps Lt. Col. John Glenn became the first American in orbit as his *Friendship* 7 circled the globe three times, a distance of 75,679 miles. The 40-year-old astronaut reached an altitude of 162.2 miles. Glenn, who flew 59 combat missions in World War II and 90 in Korea, returned to space in 1998 aboard the space shuttle *Discovery,* for a nine-day, 3.6-million-mile mission. At 77, he became history's oldest astronaut to fly in space.

The Workday

A protest turns into the disastrous Haymarket Riot, May 4, 1884.

BEFORE THE MAY 1, 1886, deadline set by the Federation of Organized Trade and Labor Unions, 10-, 12-, even 16-hour workdays were common. An eight-hour day had been proposed in 1884, but many employers were still reluctant. In Chicago, 80,000 protestors marched up Michigan Avenue. A poorly organized evening meeting on May 4 resulted in a bomb being thrown into a crowd of police who opened fire, setting off the Haymarket Riot. Unions were busted across the country. The shattered dream of an eight-hour workday didn't become a reality until the Fair Labor Standards Act of 1935.

The Death of President Lincoln

The president is shot, as pictured by an artist for *Harper's*.

FIVE DAYS AFTER THE CONCLUSION OF THE CIVIL WAR, the president and Mrs. Lincoln arrived at Ford's Theatre at 8:30 p.m. for a performance of *Our American Cousin*. It was Good Friday evening, April 14, 1865. Actor and Southern sympathizer John Wilkes Booth arrived at 9:30, then went to a bar next door. He returned to the theatre at 10:07 p.m. At 10:15 p.m., he stepped quietly into the State Box where the Lincolns sat with Henry Rathbone and his fiancée, Clara Harris. Booth fired one shot into the back of Lincoln's head, stabbed Rathbone's arm, and jumped to the stage, breaking his leg in the fall. Lincoln was taken across the street to Peterson House, but never regained consciousness. The 16th president died at 7:22 the next morning.

The Battle of Waterloo

Napoléon's last hurrah becomes a synonym for failure on a grand scale.

NAPOLÉON BONAPARTE, fresh from nine months of exile at Elba and a 100-day reign of France, invaded Belgium, attacking the Prussians at Ligny on June 16, 1815. That victory cost him 12,000 casualties. Napoléon and his 74,00 men caught up with the retreating British and other armies at Waterloo. He ordered his attack at 11:00 a.m. on June 18. At around 6:00 p.m., 40,000 British, Scot, Belgian, and German forces under the Duke of Wellington were joined by 30,000 Prussians. Bonaparte fled with his men, leaving behind 25,000 killed and wounded, and another 8,000 captured. Pursuit ceased around 9:00 p.m. This time, Napoléon would be exiled to St. Helena.

The Sinking of the *Andrea Dorea*

The *Andrea Dorea* flounders off the coast of Massachusetts.

THE $29 MILLION ITALIAN LUXURY LINER with 1,709 on board was on her 101st Atlantic crossing, en route from Genoa to New York. On the foggy night of July 25, 1956, the *Andrea Dorea* was rammed at 11:10 p.m. off Nantucket, Massachusetts, by the Swedish liner *Stockholm*. The collision killed 52, but rescue ships were able to save over 1,600 passengers and crew. The *Andrea Dorea* capsized at 10:09 the next morning.

Gertrude Ederle's English Channel Swim

Gertrude Ederle is covered in grease before attempting her historic swim.

ONLY FIVE MEN had completed the exhausting 35-mile swim before the 19-year-old New Yorker splashed into the waters of Cape Gris-Nez, France at 7:09 a.m. on August 6, 1926. Greased, determined, and ready, by afternoon she was battling not only the frigid water but wind and rain. At 9:40 p.m. she stepped ashore at Kingsdown on the British coast. Besides becoming the first woman to swim across the English Channel, she shattered the previous record by more than two hours.

D-Day

Already the bullets were zipping around these D-Day participants;
some made it to the beach and others didn't.

THE ALLIED INVASION to crack the Nazi hold on Europe had been
rumored for months. The actual invasion began before the early
morning Normandy beach landings, when the first paratroopers dropped
behind enemy lines at 01:00 the morning of June 6, 1944. Men began
loading into the landing crafts at 03:30. H-Hour, when ground forces
began landing at Omaha and Utah beaches, was 06:30. Gold and Sword
beaches came next at 07:30, followed by Juno at 07:45. All told, 160,000
troops and 30,000 vehicles landed along a 50-mile stretch. At a cost of
6,603 lives, the Normandy beachhead was finally secured at 19:30, 18-
and-one-half hours after the first parachutists landed, and 13 hours after
the first soldiers stormed the beaches.

The Last Walks on the Moon

NASA astronaut Eugene Cernan out for a moonlight drive in the Lunar Rover.

BEGINNING DECEMBER 17, 1972, when *Apollo XVII*'s lunar lander *Challenger* touched down on the moon's surface, astronauts Eugene Cernan and Harrison Schmitt collected moon rocks and performed experiments during three different ventures. Their Lunar Rover was also involved in the first lunar fender bender. This lunar stay was the longest of the *Apollo* missions, a total of 75 hours. The last manned round-trip to the moon lasted 12 days, 13 hours, and 52 minutes from December 7–19, 1972.

Strom Thurmond's Filibuster

Thurmond displays his day's worth of copy.

THURMOND'S PROTEST of the Civil Rights bill began at 8:54 p.m., August 28, 1957, with a reading of the texts of the election laws of all 48 states alphabetically from Alabama to Wyoming. The 54-year-old South Carolina senator finally took his seat at 9:12 the next evening, on the advice of his doctors who feared permanent kidney damage. Seen as the South's last hurrah against civil rights, Thurmond's effort is still the longest filibuster by one person in Senate history.

The Battle of Fort McHenry

Francis Scott Key's inspiration came during the all-night bombardment.

FRANCIS SCOTT KEY, a 35-year-old Georgetown lawyer, had come to Baltimore during the War of 1812 to secure the release of his friend, Dr. William Beanes, from the British. Key was successful in his negotiations, but was detained aboard his truce ship until after the attack on Fort McHenry. By the dawn's early light of September 14, 1814, he saw that an oversized flag dubbed "Old Glory" was still there. Putting his patriotism in his poetry, Key wrote "The Star Spangled Banner." Set to the tune of "To Anacreon in Heaven," it was officially adopted as the U.S. national anthem in 1931.

The Death of Robert F. Kennedy

The younger brother of the assassinated president announced
his candidacy in March and was buried in June.

SENATOR ROBERT F. KENNEDY, 42, had just accepted victory in the
California Democratic presidential primary in a speech at the Ambassador
Hotel in Los Angeles. As the Democratic frontrunner, he told his sup-
porters that it was time to focus their energies on the upcoming Chicago
convention. Exiting the ballroom through a pantry area, RFK was shot
three times by Sirhan Sirhan, a Palestinian Arab, at approximately
12:15 a.m., June 5, 1968. Kennedy's condition worsened throughout
the day. He was pronounced dead at 1:44 the morning of June 6.

The Chicago Fire

The great Chicago Fire began in mystery and ended in ruin.

No ONE KNOWS how the fire in the barn behind Patrick O'Leary's cottage at 137 DeKoven Street started, but the *Chicago Tribune* attributed the time as 9:30 p.m. Sunday, October 8, 1871. The first alarm sounded at 9:45 p.m. After the inferno blazed for a solid day, a Monday night rain arrived like a miracle. Smaller fires burned into the wee hours. Chicago awoke to smoke and ashes on Tuesday morning. Over 250 people died and another 98,500 were left homeless in the fire that burned 17,450 buildings.

The First Nonstop Transcontinental Flight

Kelly and Macready, ready to soar into history.

ON MAY 2, 1923, Lts. John A. Macready and Oakley G. Kelly took off from Roosevelt Field, Long Island, in a Fokker T-2 airplane. Flying mostly at night and in bad weather with only a compass and a stack of railroad maps, the pair covered 2,520 miles and reached San Diego the next day.

Lindbergh's Transatlantic Flight

"Lucky Lindy" poses next to the *Spirit of St. Louis.*

AT 7:52 A.M. ON MAY 20, 1927, in a noisy airplane named for his Missouri financial backers, Capt. Charles A. Lindbergh, 25, took off from Long Island's Roosevelt Field. Two sandwiches, 451 gallons of gasoline and 3,610 miles later, "Lucky Lindy" landed the *Spirit of St. Louis* before a crowd of 100,000 gathered at Le Bourget Field outside Paris. It was 5:22 p.m. in New York, 10:22 p.m. in Paris. Lindbergh, who hadn't slept in 55 hours, picked up a $25,000 prize for becoming the first man to fly solo over the Atlantic.

The Attack on Fort Sumter

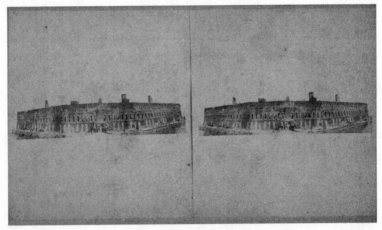

A stereopticon image of Fort Sumter.

THE CIVIL WAR BEGAN AT 4:30 a.m. on April 12, 1862, when Confederate Gen. Pierre Beauregard ordered his 4,000 men to fire upon the Union garrison at the fort in Charleston Harbor, South Carolina. Bombardment continued at intervals throughout the day and night. Maj. Robert Anderson and his 85 Union soldiers surrendered to their attackers at 2:30 p.m. the next day. Some 40,000 rounds were fired in the first battle of the war. There were no fatalities. And, in what could have been the Civil War's first sidebar, Anderson had been Beauregard's artillery instructor at West Point.

John Brown's Raid on Harper's Ferry

The fort at Harper's Ferry where John Brown made his last stand.

HOPING TO START AN ABOLITIONIST REPUBLIC in the Blue Ridge Mountains, John Brown and a group of followers seized the Federal arsenal at Harper's Ferry, West Virginia, on October 16, 1859. His dream of arming the slaves and instigating a bloody rebellion ended when U.S. Marines under Col. Robert E. Lee put down the insurrection on October 18. Brown was hanged for his crime on December 2, 1859, a martyr to his cause.

The Battle of Gettysburg

An early war photographer captures the aftermath of Gettysburg.

IT BEGAN AROUND 8:00 a.m. on July 1, 1863, when two divisions of Confederates skirmished with a Union cavalry unit west of Willoughby Run, Pennsylvania. Confederate Gen. Robert E. Lee believed he could force peace with a victory over the Army of the Potomac so far north. Union forces under Gen. George Meade defended higher ground south of Gettysburg. Hostilities ceased after 3:00 p.m. on July 3 following a disastrous rebel onslaught known as "Pickett's Charge." Lee withdrew; his Confederates reported 3,903 killed, 18,735 injured, and 5,425 missing. The Union sustained 3,155 dead, 14,529 wounded, and 5,365 missing.

The First Woman in Space

Valentina V. Tereshkova worked in a textile mill and enjoyed parachuting when she was picked to become a cosmonaut.

THE *VOSTOK 6* with 26-year-old Valentina V. Tereshkova aboard was launched into space from Baikonur at 12:29 P.M. Moscow time, June 16, 1963. During her 48 orbits, she piloted into a rendezvous with another Russian spacecraft, *Vostok 5*. Tereshkova, honored as a hero of the Soviet Union, married cosmonaut Andrian Nikolayev in November 1963. Their daughter became the first child born to parents who had both traveled in space.

The New York City Draft Riots

Violence broke out when the draft notices were posted shortly after the lists of the dead from Gettysburg had been posted.

PRESIDENT LINCOLN issued the Enrollment Act of Conscription on March 3, 1863. The first draftees were drawn July 11, one week after the horrendous Gettysburg death toll was posted. To make matters worse, wealthier draft prospects could pay a commutation fee and send someone else to do their fighting. A mob of up to 50,000 took to the streets, terrorizing, looting, burning, and lynching blacks. Lincoln sent in the Army of the Potomoc to put the riots down, but not before they claimed the lives of as many as 100 people and did $1.5 million in damages.

3 days, **19** hours, **17** minutes · **1938**

Howard Hughes's Round-the-World Flight

Howard Hughes's plane is mobbed upon landing.

IN 1937, future reclusive billionaire Howard Hughes had set a record flying across America in 7 hours, 28 minutes, 25 seconds. For this flight, he manned the controls of a Lockheed 14 twin-engine passenger plane and, with a crew of four, took off from New York's Floyd Bennett Field on July 10, 1938. He made it to Paris in half of Lindbergh's 1927 time, circled the globe, and returned to Bennett Field on July 14.

5 days • 1961

The Bay of Pigs Invasion

Confused would-be liberators study maps during their disastrous invasion of Cuba.

JOHN KENNEDY'S ADMINISTRATION got off to a bumpy start when an invasion of Cuba intended to overthrow the regime of Fidel Castro failed. Some 1,500 U.S.-trained and sponsored Cuban exiles landed at Bahía de Cochinos on April 17, 1961, after air strikes had destroyed a portion of Castro's air force. The invaders never made it to Havana. About 100 were killed. The rest were taken prisoner by Castro's army. The ill-advised invasion was a major embarrassment for the new president.

The March from Selma to Montgomery

Ralph Bunche, Ralph Abernathy, and Coretta Scott King look ahead
as Martin Luther King Jr. points the way to Montgomery.

FOLLOWING TWO EARLIER THWARTED ATTEMPTS, about 3,200 civil rights
marchers began the 44-mile march from Selma to the Alabama state capital of Montgomery on March 21, 1965. The route covered about 12 miles
a day. Participants bedded down at night in the fields along Highway 80
(also known as Jefferson Davis Highway). With 1,900 Alabama National
Guardsmen, 2,000 army personnel, U.S. marshals, and the FBI guarding
them, their numbers grew to about 25,000. Led by Dr. Martin Luther
King Jr. the group arrived at the capitol building on March 25.

The Flight of *Apollo XIII*

Apollo XIII, launched on April 11, 1970, at 1:13 p.m. (military time 13:13), entered the moon's gravitational field on April 13. Crewmembers James Lovell, Jr., John Swigert, Jr., and Fred Haise, Jr.

AT 55 HOURS AND 55 MINUTES following *Apollo XIII*'s launch to the moon, the spacecraft suffered an explosion of a service module tank. Astronauts James Lovell, John Swigart, and Fred Haise were 200,000 miles from Earth. Swigert radioed back, "Okay, Houston, we've had a problem here." They had lost their normal supply of electricity, light, and water. Capsule temperatures dropped to 38 degrees, and the moon mission was aborted. The world watched for the next three-and-one-half days as the crippled craft circled around the moon and made a successful but perilous return to Earth.

The Stock Market Crash

The panic sets in. New York's Wall Street is a scene
of mass bewilderment as the market collapses.

THE DOWNTREND turned to outright panic on Black Thursday, October
24, 1929, when over 12 million shares changed hands at the New York
Stock Exchange. Selling hysteria began again on Monday, with Tuesday,
October 29, bringing the total crash with 16 million shares sold. The president
of Union Cigar saw his stock plummet from $113.50 to $4 in one
day. Whether he fell or jumped from his hotel ledge was never determined,
but it became a common belief that big losers were jumping out
of Wall Street windows. On paper, $30 billion in stocks evaporated over
the next three weeks. By 1933, 13 million Americans were out of work.

The Bataan Death March

Participants of the Bataan Death March, where asking for a drink of water could get you killed.

ON APRIL 9, 1942, 78,000 American and Filipino defenders of Bataan in the Philippines surrendered to the Japanese. Many POWs were executed immediately. Survivors, deprived of food and water, were then force-marched through 65 miles of jungle from Mariveles to San Fernando. Over 5,000 Americans died on the march. On April 15, those who could still walk were loaded into boxcars and shipped to Camp O'Donnell. The remaining prisoners, 9,300 American and 45,000 Filipino, were subjected to unusual cruelty, including daily beatings and beheadings. This episode of World War II was so brutal that details were kept secret for two years.

The Watts Riots

The long, hot summer of 1965 erupts in Watts.

WHAT SHOULD HAVE BEEN a routine drunk-driving arrest in Los Angeles on the evening of August 11, 1965, turned into one of the worst riots in U.S. history. On a too-hot summer night, a crowd gathered around the LAPD officers who had stopped a 21-year-old black motorist just after 7:00 p.m. Almost instantly the situation escalated into full-scale violence over a 46-square-mile area. Some 35,000 people rioted, while 16,000 National Guardsmen were called in. By the time the looting and burning ceased on August 16, there were 34 dead, 4,100 in jail, and 200 demolished buildings. Damages were estimated at about $200 million.

The Six-Day War

Israeli troops in Jerusalem: a 132-and-a-half-hour war changes everything.

TENSIONS PITTING EGYPT, SYRIA, AND JORDAN against Israel culminated in an Israeli attack that destroyed 400 Egyptian combat aircraft on June 5, 1967. After four days of fighting with Egyptian forces, Israel occupied the Sinai Peninsula (from Egypt) and the Golan Heights (from Syria). Jordan attacked Jerusalem but was repelled. Fighting with Syria in the Golan Heights ceased on June 10, the day all countries involved accepted the U.N. Security Council's cease-fire at 16:30 GMT. The war claimed 759 Israelis and over 15,000 Arabs.

The Death of President McKinley

Czolgosz shoots President McKinley with a concealed revolver at the Pan-American Exposition reception, September 6, 1901.

PRESIDENT MCKINLEY attended the Pan-American Exposition in Buffalo, New York, on Friday, September 6, 1901. At a reception at 4:07 p.m., he was approached by a man with a bandaged hand. Wrapped in the gauze was a .32-caliber Johnson revolver. An anarchist from Cleveland named Leon Czolgosz, 28, fired twice. McKinley, 58, lingered until 2:16 a.m. on September 14. He was the third president to be assassinated in 36 years. Czolgosz was electrocuted on October 29, 1901, one month, 15 days after the president's death.

The Scopes Monkey Trial

The confrontation between Clarence Darrow and William Jennings Bryan would fuel the play *Inherit the Wind,* and later the movie of the same name.

HIGH SCHOOL BIOLOGY TEACHER JOHN SCOPES, 24, was charged with illegally teaching the evolution theories of Charles Darwin at Dayton, Tennessee. Three-time presidential candidate William Jennings Bryan, 65, joined the prosecution on May 30, 1925. Clarence Darrow, 69, agreed to defend Scopes. Proceedings were called to order July 10, 1925. On the seventh day, in what the *New York Times* described as "the most amazing court scene in Anglo-Saxon history," Bryan took the stand as an expert on the Bible and was grilled by Darrow. The carnival-like atmosphere culminated in a guilty verdict, with a hand slap of a $100 fine. Five days after the trial ended, William Jennings Bryan died.

The Battle of the Alamo

The defenders of the Alamo are overrun by Santa Anna's troops.

A REBELLION BY TEXAS SETTLERS against the government of Mexico had escalated into the Texas War of Independence. Some 189 pioneers (including William Barrett Travis, James Bowie, and Davy Crockett) took refuge in a 118-year-old Franciscan mission in San Antonio, Texas. On February 24, 1836, a day after their arrival, some 5,000 troops under Mexican President Antonio López de Santa Anna laid siege. Around 5:00 a.m. March 6, his forces breeched the walls and killed all the defenders in about three hours. Santa Anna lost over 1,500 men. He was later defeated by Gen. Sam Houston's forces at the Battle of San Jacinto. Their battle cry? "Remember the Alamo!"

13 days · **1962**

The Cuban Missile Crisis

MRBM LAUNCH SITE 2
SAN CRISTOBAL
1 NOVEMBER 1962

FUEL TRAILERS

MISSILE READY TENT

FORMER LAUNCH POSITIONS

FORMER LOCATION OF MISSILE READY TENTS

Soviet missile sites in Cuba triggered the crisis in 1962.

THE COLD WAR almost turned thermonuclear when an American U-2 reconnaissance aircraft discovered several SS-4 nuclear missiles in Castro's Cuba. Days of secret meetings followed, after which President Kennedy informed the American people of the military buildup on October 22, 1962. In language directed at Soviet Premier Nikita Kruschev, Kennedy warned that "any nuclear missile launched from Cuba against any nation in the Western Hemisphere ... would require a full retaliatory attack." Tense days followed, during which the U.S. imposed a military blockade around Cuba. In an October 28 address on Radio Moscow, Kruschev announced that the missiles would be removed.

The Declaration of Independence

A hard deadline for an historic document.

THE CONTINENTAL CONGRESS selected a committee—John Adams, Benjamin Franklin, Thomas Jefferson, Robert R. Livingston, and Roger Sherman—to draft a document proclaiming the split of the 13 original colonies from Great Britain. The committee chose Jefferson to be the author. He began work on June 11, 1776, composing several drafts before returning the document to his breakout group. They in turn made their revisions and presented the finished product on June 28. Congress made their changes, then released it on July 4, 1776.

Survival of the First Successful Heart Transplant

A nine-hour operation makes history.

DR. CHRISTIAAN BARNARD performed the surgery on Louis Washkansky, 55, at the Groote Schuur Hospital in Cape Town, South Africa, on December 3, 1967. Washkansky survived the operation, in which he received the heart of Denise Darvall, 25, who had been struck by a car. Washkansky contracted pneumonia, however, and died on December 21.

The Siege of Yorktown

The men under Cornwallis literally laid down their arms, effectively ending the Revolutionary War.

THE CLIMACTIC VICTORY of the Revolution occurred when Gen. George Washington's force of 9,000 American and French soldiers were joined by troops under the Marquis de Lafayette, bringing their total to 17,600 men. Gen. Charles Cornwallis and his 5,000 British soldiers were trapped on Chesapeake Bay at Yorktown, Virginia, on September 28, 1781. Weary of fighting and unaware that reinforcements were on the way, the British army laid down their arms and Cornwallis surrendered October 20. The surrender was complete, as was the last major battle of the Revolutionary War.

Handel Composes *Messiah*

A formal portrait of Handel, who originally intended his oratorio for the Easter season.

GEORGE FRIDERIC HANDEL, 56, had been partially paralyzed from a recent stroke. He credited divine inspiration for his feverish pace that lasted from August 22 to September 14, 1741. During that time he never left his house on Brook Street in London; meals delivered were often left uneaten. Found in tears while he composed the "Hallelujah Chorus," Handel said, "I did think I did see all Heaven before me and the great God himself." The world premiere of the 260 pages of music came in Dublin, Ireland, April 13, 1742.

The Shortest Presidency

William Henry Harrison as depicted by lithographer Charles Fenderich in 1841. His inauguration speech, at 8,443 words, was the longest. His term in office was the shortest.

THE NINTH AMERICAN PRESIDENT, William Henry Harrison, 68, insisted on a 100-minute speech at his outdoor inauguration on March 4, 1841. Having campaigned as a tough Indian fighter, the former governor of the Illinois Territory refused coat, hat, and gloves. The cold he caught at the event progressed to pneumonia by March 27. He became the first president to die in office on April 4, 1841.

Deciding the 2000 Presidential Election

Dan Rather said, "This election is shakier than cafeteria Jell-O."

NO SOONER HAD THE FOX NETWORK called the November 7, 2000, election for George W. Bush (2:16 a.m., November 8, 2000) than the outcome was plunged into doubt. Numerous voting discrepancies were found in the must-win state of Florida. Dimpled chads, butterfly ballots, manual recounts, and heavyweight legal maneuverings became the order of the nightly news as the pendulum of history swayed back and forth between the camps of Republican Bush and Democrat Al Gore. At 9:54 p.m. on December 12, the U.S. Supreme Court reversed a recount decision by the Florida Supreme Court, and Bush was declared the winner of that state's electoral votes. Gore conceded December 13.

The Persian Gulf War

President George Herbert Walker Bush and his advisers hear a White House briefing from Gen. Colin Powell.

CITING OIL OVERPRODUCTION as a form of economic warfare against his country, Iraq's Saddam Hussein invaded Kuwait on August 2, 1990. A U.N. embargo came four days later. An international coalition turned Operation Desert Shield into Desert Storm on January 17, 1991, at 2:38 a.m. Baghdad time. A total of 850 bombing missions were carried out over the Iraqi capital in the initial 48 hours. The first scud missile struck Israel January 18. The ground war began on February 24 and was over in 100 hours. Kuwait City was liberated on February 27, 1991, and the cease-fire took effect at 8:00 a.m. on February 28.

The First U.S. Transcontinental Flight

Calbraith Perry Rodgers, 32, on the Chicago leg of his trip.

CALBRAITH PERRY RODGERS, 32, became the first person to accomplish the feat, motivated by a $50,000 prize offered by publishing tycoon William Randolph Hearst. Rodgers took off in the *Vin Fiz* from Sheepshead Bay, New York, on September 17, 1911, landing 70 times and crashing 16 times before arriving in Pasadena, California, on November 5, which technically completed the transcontinental flight. On December 10 he flew the craft on to Long Beach so he could make it all the way to the Pacific. In that time he was only in the air for 82 hours and four minutes.

The Court-Martial of Billy Mitchell

Billy Mitchell stands during his court proceedings.

BRIG. GEN. WILLIAM MITCHELL was a pilot in World War I, after which he became a major booster for air power, convinced that it would make ground and naval battles things of the past. In 1925, Mitchell publicly blasted the army and navy for their failure to see the benefits of military aviation. A court-martial for insubordination began October 28, 1925. All but one of the 13 officers who judged him—Douglas MacArthur— found him guilty on December 17, suspending his rank and command and revoking his pay for five years. Billy Mitchell resigned from the military on February 1, 1926, and spent the rest of his life promoting the necessity of air superiority in defense and in war.

Reaching the South Pole

Amundsen's men erect shelter at the South Pole.

HAVING STARTED FROM THE BAY OF WHALES on October 18, 1911, Norwegian Roald Amundsen along with Olav Olavson Bjaaland, Hilmer Hanssen, Sverre H. Hassel, Oscar Wisting, and 11 dogs became the first to reach the South Pole at 3:00 p.m. on December 14. All made it back to their base camp safely 99 days and 1,860 miles later on January 25, 1912. A five-man party led by Robert Falcon Scott arrived at the pole on January 18, 1912, only to find they had been beaten by Amundsen's crew. The Scott expedition perished on the return trip.

The Army–McCarthy Hearings

Roy Cohn and Joseph McCarthy during the hearings.

WISCONSIN SENATOR JOSEPH McCARTHY's Communist witch hunt was presented in living black and white on the infant medium of television. McCarthy zeroed in on the army as a haven for Reds in hearings that began in the Senate Caucus Room April 22, 1954. During 188 hours of coverage, an estimated 20 million Americans beheld the man who would out all Communists, real or imagined. On June 9, Boston attorney Joseph Welch delivered his famous line, "Have you no sense of decency, sir, at long last? Have you no sense of decency?" By adjournment on June 17, McCarthy's act had worn thin. The Senate voted to condemn him the following December.

The Impeachment of President Clinton

President Clinton in happier times.

OVER A YEAR OF ACCUSATIONS and denials culminated in William Jefferson Clinton, 42, the 42nd president, becoming the second president in American history to endure an impeachment proceeding. On December 11, 1998, the House Judiciary Committee passed three impeachment articles accusing the president of lying to a grand jury, committing perjury by denying he had sexual relations with Monica Lewinsky, and obstructing justice. On December 19, the House of Representatives voted to impeach the president on the perjury and obstruction of justice charges. A 36-day Senate trial, beginning January 7, 1999, resulted in an acquittal on both charges on February 12, 1999.

The Atlantic Voyage of the *Mayflower*

The *Mayflower* alone on the great ocean, from a 19th-century engraving.

A CREW OF 102 PILGRIMS onboard the *Mayflower* left England on September 6, 1620, on a voyage to the New World and religious freedom. Their destination was Virginia, but on November 9 they sighted land first at Cape Cod. Although the transatlantic part of the journey was over, they had yet to find a place to settle. On November 11 they anchored at what is today Provincetown, where the male passengers signed the "Mayflower Compact." It wasn't until December 16 that the *Mayflower* arrived at Plymouth Harbor, where construction on the settlement began December 23. The first Thanksgiving was celebrated the following autumn.

The First Voyage of Columbus

Artist's conception of the Columbus landing.

CHRISTOPHER COLUMBUS, 41, thought that by sailing west he would run into the islands in the China Sea described by 12th century traveler Marco Polo. A crew of 88 aboard the *Niña,* the *Pinta,* and the *Santa Maria* departed from Palos, Spain, on August 3, 1492. The voyage was stalled by calm winds and repairs for four weeks in the Canary Islands. It resumed September 6, averaging 150 miles a day. Ten days later, what looked like land turned out to be the Sargasso Sea. When birds were sighted flying southwest on October 8, Columbus changed his course. At 2:00 a.m. October 12, lookout Rodrigo de Tirana on the *Pinta* spotted the moon glistening off a Bahamian shore. The ships docked on an island the native Tainos called Guanahani. Columbus renamed it San Salvador.

Nellie Bly's Trip Around the World

A souvenir postcard commemorates the globetrotting antics of Nellie Bly.

BLY WAS THE PEN NAME of *New York World* journalist Elizabeth Cochrane. Inspired by Jules Verne's *Around the World in 80 Days,* she convinced her publisher, Joseph Pulitzer, to fund a mission for a woman to break the fictitious feat. Pulitzer went for it, and a million people entered a contest to guess the outcome of her journey. Nellie departed from Hoboken at 9:40 a.m., November 14, 1889, and was back in New York at 3:40 p.m. January 25, 1890. (Bly's calculations—total tour time, 1,734 hours and 11 minutes; average rate of speed, including stops 28.71 mph. "I spent 56 days, 12 hours, and 41 minutes in actual travel and lost by delay 15 days, 17 hours, 30 minutes.")

The Disappearance of the Lindbergh Baby

EXTRA DAILY MIRROR **EXTRA**

LINDY'S BABY MURDERED!

The worst that could happen is realized.

THE LONE EAGLE'S FIRST CHILD, Charles Lindbergh, Jr., three months shy of his second birthday, was kidnapped from his bedroom at Lindbergh's Hopewell, New Jersey, estate the night of March 1, 1932. Police found a badly spelled ransom note. A shocked country followed the ordeal of Lindbergh and his wife, Anne Morrow, in lurid daily headlines. The nightmare scenario reached the worst conclusion when the baby's remains were discovered not far from the family property on May 12. The media circus was not over; a lengthy trial resulted in the execution of Bruno Hauptmann on April 3, 1936.

The Death of President Garfield

The Garfield shooting as it appeared in the CNN of its day, Frank Leslie's illustrated newspaper, July 16, 1881.

ON THE 120TH DAY of his administration, July 2, 1881, the 20th president, James Abram Garfield, 49, was shot at the Washington, D.C., train depot by deranged attorney Charles Guiteau. The first physician to seek the bullet probed the wound with his finger and nonsterile instruments. Alexander Graham Bell's metal detector sent surgeons in the direction of a bedspring. As infection set in, no fewer than 16 doctors failed to find the bullet, widening the wound from three to 20 inches. Garfield dropped 80 pounds and had a heart attack before dying on the evening of September 19, 1881. Despite a defense that blamed the president's doctors, Guiteau was hanged on June 30, 1882.

FDR's First 100 Days

A confident president is also the last to ever take the oath of office in March.

The 32nd president, Franklin Delano Roosevelt, 51, declared there was "nothing to fear but fear itself" in his March 4, 1933, inauguration address. From there he set out to prove it to a Depression-weary nation. He called Congress into a special 100-day session (March 9–June 16), stopped all gold trading, and called for a nationwide bank holiday until the panic subsided. To combat a $5 billion deficit, he cut a half billion from the budget. Congress legitimized beer and a half million workers went back to work. Farm incomes improved with the Agriculture Adjustment Act. The New Deal also included the Civilian Conservation Corps, which put millions of Americans back to work and helped the environment.

The Spanish-American War

American soldiers fighting in the Philippines.

IN 1895, GUERILLA WAR BROKE OUT as Cuba sought independence from Spain. Presidents Cleveland and McKinley unsuccessfully sought diplomatic resolutions. War fever peaked when the U.S. battleship *Maine* exploded in Havana harbor February 15, 1898, killing 260. McKinley asked Congress to declare war April 11, 1898, and on April 19 armed intervention was authorized. Cuban ports were blockaded, and Admiral Dewey defeated the Spanish fleet at Manila Bay in the Philippines. Teddy Roosevelt led his Rough Riders up San Juan Hill July 1, after which Spain sued for peace and an armistice was signed August 12. The Treaty of Paris, signed December 10, 1898, freed Cuba, gave the United States possession of Puerto Rico and Guam, and arranged for the United States to purchase the Philippines for $20 million.

The Salem Witch Trials

The naked truth. Another witch is discovered in Salem.

WITCH HYSTERIA began in Massachusetts January 10, 1692, when Elizabeth Parris, nine, and Abigail Williams, 11, displayed odd behavior. A diagnosis of Satanic influence came from physicians in February, soon after the girls identified three witches, including the slave Tituba. Accusations flew. The Court of Oyer and Terminer was convened on June 2, and on June 10 they hanged their first witch, Bridget Bishop. Over the next few months 13 women and five men were put to death. Gov. William Phipps called a halt to the proceedings on October 29 when he dissolved the court.

The First Around-the-World Flight

Crewmembers on their historic journey pose for a group shot at the
Croydon Aerodrome near London.

FOUR SPECIALLY BUILT military Douglas World Cruisers, each with a two-
man crew, departed westward from Seattle, Washington, on April 6, 1924,
attempting the first flights to circumnavigate the globe. A storm at Dutch
Harbor, Alaska, claimed the *Seattle*. The mission of the *Boston* ended with a
forced landing in the Atlantic. The two remaining planes, dubbed *Chicago*
and *New Orleans,* completed the feat, some 26,345 total miles in 363 flying
hours over 175 days, returning to Seattle on September 28.

The London Blitz

A glimpse of St. Paul's Cathedral through the smoke during the raid of December 29, 1940.

BOMBS FROM THE FIRST OF SOME 70 ATTACKS hit central London August 24, 1940, damaging St. Giles Church, Cripplegate. Great Britain responded with bombings around Berlin. The blitz itself commenced after dark September 7 when 300 German bombers escorted by 600 fighters unloaded 337 tons of bombs on London, igniting 1,000 fires, killing 430, and injuring 1,600. By mid-October, a quarter of a million British had been blasted out of their homes. On April 16, 1941, over a thousand people were killed in a raid by 685 bombers. The worst night was May 10, 1941, when 700 tons of bombs and thousands of incendiaries killed over 1,500 people. Night raids were frequent through May 1941.

Viking 1's Voyage to Mars

It may look like a lonesome chunk of west Texas, but it is the first close-up view of the Martian landscape from *Viking 1*. The Chryse Planitia, "Plains of Gold," July 20, 1976.

ON AUGUST 20, 1975, the *Viking 1* was launched by NASA on a mission to Mars. Once in Martian orbit, it sought a place to land. On July 20, 1976, the *Viking 1* lander touched down at Chryse Planitia. The *Viking 2* lander arrived at Utopia Planitia on September 3, 1976, after a voyage of 11 months, 26 days. The two orbiters imaged the entire surface of Mars before they were powered down in 1978 and 1980. The *Viking 2* lander's work ended in 1980, while the original *Viking 1* lander communicated until November 13, 1982. The two transmitted some 1,400 images in over six years on Mars.

The Montgomery Bus Boycott

Rosa Parks is booked and fingerprinted. Her famous
bus ride would trigger the Montgomery boycott.

SEAMSTRESS ROSA PARKS, 42, was arrested in Montgomery, Alabama, for
refusing to relinquish her bus seat to a white rider on December 1, 1955.
She was found guilty and fined $14, an amount she refused to pay. Upset
community leaders believed a boycott could be an instrument of change,
since 25,000 African American residents made up 75 percent of the city's
bus patrons. Dexter Avenue Baptist Church pastor, Martin Luther King Jr.
was asked to lead the Montgomery Improvement Association in a movement to end discrimination as well as demand better treatment for passengers and jobs for black drivers. The boycott started December 5, 1955,
and ran until after the Supreme Court voted that public transportation
segregation was in violation of federal law, December 21, 1956.

John Dillinger's Crime Spree

Tension reigns as Dillinger accounts for more sensational headlines.

IN HIS LAST YEAR, John Dillinger, Public Enemy Number One, robbed at least 11 banks and had numerous gun battles with police, creating panic throughout the Midwest. After completing a nine-year prison stay for robbery May 22, 1934, he quickly made up for lost time. Six fast robberies began June 10, 1933, at New Carlisle, Ohio, and concluded with a $75,000 haul at Greencastle, Indiana. After the gang was arrested January 25, 1934, in Tucson, Arizona, Dillinger was extradited for killing a Chicago policeman. He escaped waving a wooden gun on March 3, 1934. A final robbery at South Bend, Indiana, netted $30,000 on June 30, 1934. Working on a tip, authorities found Dillinger emerging from Chicago's Biograph Theatre July 22, 1934, and gunned him down. He was 31 years old.

Empire State Building Construction

Modern technology prevails during the depths of the depression.

THE TALLEST BUILDING IN THE WORLD for over 40 years, the Empire State Building was a marvel of Depression-era genius. The 102-story, 1,250-foot skyscraper was built by a workforce of 3,000 who put in 7 million man hours with no overtime. Designed by architect William Lamb, construction began March 17, 1930. The 58,000-ton frame rose four-and-one-half floors a week and was riveted together in just 23 weeks. Plumbers installed 51 miles of pipe, electricians hooked up 17 million feet of telephone wire, and masons completed the exterior in eight months. On May 1, 1931, with the press of a button at the White House, President Herbert Hoover officially lit and opened the Empire State Building.

American Hostages in Iran

A hostage is paraded before the cameras.

ON NOVEMBER 4, 1979, some 3,000 militants took over the U.S. embassy in Tehran in an attempt to have the former shah, Mohammad Reza Pahlavi, hospitalized in the United States, returned to Iran to face a death sentence. President Jimmy Carter refused and froze Iranian assets. The worsening crisis remained the top spot on the nightly news and figured heavily in Carter's loss to Ronald Reagan. Behind-the-scenes negotiations arranged for a thaw of Iranian assets, a freeze on the late shah's wealth (he had died the previous July), a lift of trade restrictions, and a promise to stay out of Iranian affairs. The Ayatollah Khomeini ordered the 52 hostages released on their 444th day in captivity, right after Reagan's inauguration, January 20, 1981.

O. J. Simpson's Jail Stay

When it was finally over, O.J. didn't run, he walked.

KNOWN FOR HIS PROWESS on the gridiron and his success as a TV pitchman, Orenthal James Simpson was charged in the double homicide of his wife, Nicole Brown Simpson, and Ron Goldman on June 17, 1994, five days after the killings. The trial began January 24, 1995, and quickly turned into a media circus starring Marcia Clark and Christopher Darden for the prosecution and a dream team led by Johnnie Cochran for the defense. It eventually broke the California record trial length previously set by the Manson family proceedings. Simpson's acquittal came on his 474th day in jail from a jury sequestered for 266 days on October 3, 1995.

The Lewinsky Affair

Lurid headlines fuel the White House scandal.

MONICA LEWINSKY, 21, joined the White House staff as an unpaid intern in Leon Panetta's office in June 1995. On November 15, she began a relationship with President Clinton. In December, she moved to a paid position with the Office of Legislative Affairs. Her last intimate encounter with the president took place March 29, 1997. Transferring to the Pentagon in April 1997, she met government worker Linda Tripp, who began recording their conversations in the autumn of 1997. Lewinsky talked briefly with Clinton on her last visit to the White House on December 28, 11 days after she had been subpoenaed by lawyers for Paula Jones. Clinton's famous denial came January 26, 1998.

The Pony Express

In this symbolic depiction, a Pony Express rider hails the builders
of the transcontinental telegraph.

DELIVERING THE MAIL RELAY FASHION on horseback across the vast
expanses of the West was the brainchild of expressmen William Russell,
Alexander Majors, and W. B. Waddell. Some 190 stations were scattered
across a 1,966-mile trail from St. Joseph, Missouri, to Sacramento,
California. The first rider rode out of St. Joe at 7:15 p.m. April 3, 1860;
the final rider on the stretch arrived in Sacramento April 13. Expensive
postage (about $5 for a half-ounce) and the coming of the transconti-
nental telegraph spelled an end to the service that delivered 34,753
pieces of mail over 650,000 miles during its brief existence.

The Captivity of Patty Hearst

Tanya (Patty Hearst) in full battle dress.

ON FEBRUARY 4, 1974, Patricia Randolph Hearst, 19, a student at Berkeley, was kidnapped by the Symbionese Liberation Army. Before her ordeal concluded, the granddaughter of publishing tycoon William Randolph Hearst became a wanted fugitive and participated in the Hibernia Bank robbery in San Francisco on April 15. The FBI caught her September 18, 1975. F. Lee Bailey defended the robbery charge but a jury found her guilty March 11, 1976. She was sentenced to seven years in prison and was released February 1, 1979, when President Carter commuted her debt to society to time served.

The Mexican War

A lithograph by German artist Carl Nebel, who witnessed Gen. Winfield
Scott's troops entering Mexico City on September 14, 1847.

MEXICO HAD REFUSED TO SELL CALIFORNIA and other regions to the
United States. Further complicating matters was Texas, owned by Mexico,
homesteaded by Americans, and finally annexed by the United States in
1845. Mexican soldiers won a skirmish north of the Rio Grande on April
24, 1846, prompting the United States to declare war May 13. Northern
Mexico and California were invaded, resulting in American victories at
Palo Alto, Resaca de la Palma, Monterrey, and Buena Vista. Gen. Winfield
Scott's troops entered Mexico City September 14, 1847, and occupied it
until peace was negotiated. The Treaty of Guadalupe Hidalgo, signed
March 10, 1848, authorized a U.S. payment to Mexico of $15 million
in exchange for about half of its territory.

Elvis in the Army

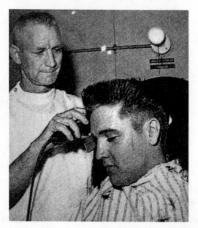

The sideburns weren't exactly regulation. Elvis Presley gets a
dreaded haircut before becoming a celebrity soldier.

THE KING OF ROCK AND ROLL had a blue Christmas thanks to some
fan mail he received from Uncle Sam December 10, 1957. Granted a
60-day extension to film *King Creole,* Elvis subsequently reported to his
draft board March 24, 1958. GI blues set in as his income dropped from
$400,000 to $78.00 a month. He left basic training at Fort Hood, Texas,
in August to attend the funeral of his mother, Gladys Presley. Then he
and his unit were shipped to Weisbaden, Germany. After moving up to
the rank of corporal, Elvis returned for his honorable discharge at Fort
Dix, New Jersey, March 5, 1960. He weighed 185 pounds when he went
in and 170 pounds when he was released.

Building Hoover Dam

Nevada's Hoover Dam was truly an all-American product.
Every state in the union contributed supplies and materials.

The diversion of the Colorado River began in 1932, but the actual construction of Hoover Dam began on June 6, 1933, when workmen laid the first concrete. The 726.4-foot-high dam required up to 10,800 barrels of cement a day, a total of 5 million barrels in all. The maximum workforce of 5,218 was reached in June 1934. The last concrete was laid on May 29, 1935. Upon completion, the dam weighed 6.6 million tons. According to one estimate, if Hoover Dam had been built with 100-pound blocks laid every minute, day and night, it would have taken from the time of the Pilgrims (1620) until the Great Depression of the 1930s to complete.

The Diary of Anne Frank

Dit is een foto, zoals
ik me zou wensen,
altijd zo te zijn.
Dan had ik nog wel
een kans om naar
Holywood te komen.
Anne Frank
10 Oct. 1942

(translation)
"This is a photo as I would wish
myself to look all the time. Then
I would maybe have a chance to
come to Hollywood."
Anne Frank, 10 Oct. 1942

Most likely to be remembered.

ANNE FRANK'S FATHER gave her the diary for her 13th birthday, June 12, 1942; she made the first entry that day. Three weeks later, July 6, 1942, she and her family went into hiding in "the Secret Annexe" adjacent to Mr. Frank's former office in Amsterdam. The Van Daan family joined them July 13. Her final entry was penned August 1, 1944, three days before the group was found and arrested by secret police. She died of typhus at age 15 in March 1945, in Germany's Bergen-Belsen concentration camp. Only her father, Otto, survived the death camps; he found the diary when he returned to the hideout in 1947.

The Watergate Scandal

The Nixons bid farewell to the Fords following
the resignation, August 9, 1974.

"THE LONG NATIONAL NIGHTMARE" as Gerald Ford dubbed it, began with
the arrest of five former CIA employees trying to bug the offices of the
Democratic National Committee in Washington's Watergate Hotel at
2:30 a.m., June 17, 1972. A supposed botched burglary quickly evolved
into a hurricane-level political scandal. A Senate Select Committee convened televised hearings February 7, 1973. The nightly news filled with
tales of "dirty tricks," "stonewalling," "expletives deleted," and the search
for a "smoking gun." The scandal consumed top White House staff members, and eventually, on August 9, 1974, President Richard Nixon himself.

The Lewis and Clark Expedition

A skirmish with Piegan Blackfeet on the return trip. Lewis killed a member of a band that had stolen supplies and horses.

IN 1803, PRESIDENT THOMAS JEFFERSON picked his personal secretary, Meriwether Lewis, to lead a Western expedition across the newly acquired Louisiana Purchase. Lewis chose William Clark as his second in command and began recruiting crewmembers and assembling supplies. At 4:00 p.m., May 14, 1804, the Corps of Discovery departed Camp Dubois, just upstream from St. Louis, and headed across present Kansas and Nebraska. While wintering north of present Bismarck, North Dakota, they hired Toussaint Charbonneau as an interpreter. With him came his teen bride, the indispensable guide Sacagawea. The westward trek continued April 7, 1805. They reached Gray's Bay, 20 miles from the Pacific Ocean, on November 7 and made winter camp on November 24. The return trip to St. Louis took from March 23 to September 23, 1806.

The Siege of Leningrad

A shot from inside the city under siege.

HITLER'S TROOPS surrounded the Russian city September 8, 1941, cutting off the defending Soviet troops and 2,877,000 civilians (including almost a half-million children) from the rest of the world. A 60-day supply of food and fuel had to last 871 days. Over 200,000 people died of starvation and bitter cold in the first two months of 1942. Still, the relentless shelling continued. Many escaped the city during the warm seasons, and supplies were smuggled in over Lake Ladoga, but still, when the blockade was finally broken January 27, 1944, the death toll was staggering. A total of 641,000 had died in Leningrad, the city that refused to surrender.

The War of 1812

Andrew Jackson directs American forces at the Battle of New
Orleans. A copy of an engraving by H. B. Hall after W. Momberger.

"AMERICA'S SECOND WAR OF INDEPENDENCE" began when the United
States declared war on Great Britain June 18, 1812, over violations of
American neutrality. The U.S. invasion of Canada was a bust, but Perry's
victory at Lake Erie and Harrison's successful Battle of the Thames
secured the Northwest in 1813. The following year the British invaded
and burned Washington, D.C. Peace came with the Treaty of Ghent on
December 24, 1814, but the word failed to reach New Orleans, where
Andrew Jackson's command scored the greatest American land victory
of the war two weeks after it was over.

---

*The time is from the declaration of war until the signing of the peace—Jackson's victory
happened after the war ended.

Drake's Circumnavigation of the Globe

Artist Marcus Gheeraerts the Younger
captured Drake on canvas in 1591.

ON DECEMBER 13, 1577, Sir Francis Drake sailed with five ships from
Plymouth, England. He lost four ships in the 330-mile Straits of Magellan,
but continued on in the *Golden Hind*. Sailing north up the coast of South
America, Drake raided Spanish settlements and ships along the way. He
spent five weeks probably around present San Francisco, then headed
west, crossing the Pacific and Indian Oceans and finally rounding the tip
of Africa into the Atlantic, arriving back in England September 26, 1580.
Queen Elizabeth I knighted the first Englishman to sail around the world
the next year.

The Manhattan Project

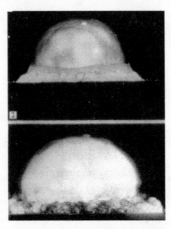

A fire in the desert—the atomic bomb
test of July 16, 1945.

PRESIDENT FRANKLIN ROOSEVELT gave the go-ahead to build the atomic
bomb on October 9, 1941. On December 6, the day before Pearl Harbor
was attacked, he authorized the Manhattan Engineering District to
create it. The real work began when Brig. Gen. Leslie Groves was put in
charge of the project September 17, 1942, and J. Robert Oppenheimer
became the scientific director. The project commenced in Hanford,
Washington; Oak Ridge, Tennessee; and Los Alamos, New Mexico.
Over 120,000 people worked in some capacity on the $2 billion under-
taking. The first atom bomb was successfully tested at the Trinity site
at Alamagordo, New Mexico, on July 16, 1945.

Influenza Pandemic

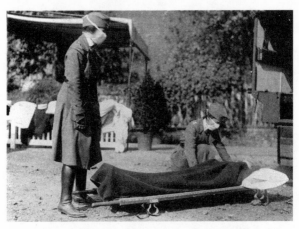

Nurses give a demonstration in how to combat the flu pandemic at the Red Cross Emergency Ambulance Station in Washington, D.C.

CHICAGO'S CRIME RATE dropped 43 percent. In one day, 851 New Yorkers died. More American soldiers died of the "Spanish flu" in 1918 than were killed on the battlefields of World War I. Since epidemic bronchitis preceded the flu from 1915 to 1917 in France and England, few individuals had a prior immunity to this new lethal strain and often died within a week of exposure. In the United States, 500,000 deaths were recorded between March and November of 1918. Globally, about 40 million people died. Recent studies say the virus may have percolated within humans and pigs for several years until it grew lethal enough to emerge as history's worst influenza pandemic.

The Korean War

Crossing the 38th parallel.

COMMUNIST FORCES from North Korea crossed the 38th parallel and invaded South Korea on June 25, 1950. The United Nations authorized the United States and other countries to send military aid two days later. President Truman committed ground troops on June 30. The war eventually involved Gen. Douglas MacArthur's invasion of North Korea, the entry of China into the fray, and the removal of MacArthur from his command. An armistice was signed July 27, 1953. The United Nations tallied 550,000 casualties, including 95,000 dead. American losses included 33,686 killed and 103,284 wounded. The opposing forces had 1.5 million casualties, of whom 900,000 were Chinese.

The Civil War

America's fascination with the Civil War continues today. Over 65,000 books have been published on the subject since the war ended in 1865.

THE CONFLICT between the states in the North and South simmered for years over many disagreements, primarily over slavery and states' rights. Between the election and inauguration of Abraham Lincoln, seven states began the Confederacy by seceding from the Union. War began with the shelling of Fort Sumter, South Carolina, April 12, 1861, and ended with the surrender by Robert E. Lee to Ulysses S. Grant at the Appomattox Court House in Virginia April 9, 1865. In between, 3 million men fought the war on historic battlefields including Gettysburg, Vicksburg, Antietam, and Chickamauga. Over 620,000 people, 2 percent of the population, gave their lives.

The Black Death

A Flemish miniature from 1349 showing massive funerals
as a result of the plague.

THE PLAGUE FIRST ARRIVED from the Crimea in October of 1347 on
twelve rat-infested merchant ships from Caffa that docked at Genoa,
Italy. Terrified people fled from city to city, helping to spread the plague
across the continent. It reached Marseilles, France, in January 1348 and
Great Britain through the southern coastal ports the following
September. From there, over the winter of 1349, it spread to Scotland,
Wales, and Ireland. Death toll estimates vary, anywhere from one-tenth to
one-third of the population. This first encounter of the plague ended in
Scandinavia in 1351. It returned again in 1365, and many times thereafter.

World War I

Marine receiving first aid before being sent to hospital in rear of trenches. Photo taken in the Toulon Sector, France, March 22, 1918, by Sgt. Leon H. Caverly, USMC.

THE MAIN EVENT that precipitated the Great War was the assassination of Archduke Franz Ferdinand and his wife Sophie in Sarajevo, June 28, 1914. On July 28, Austria-Hungary declared war on Serbia. Germany aligned with Austria-Hungary against Great Britain, France, and Russia. The entry of the United States with their declaration of war on Germany, April 6, 1917, solidified the first global conflict. Over 2 million U.S. doughboys joined in the fighting over the next 16 months. The conflict ceased with the Armistice on November 11, 1918. The Treaty of Versailles was signed June 28, 1919, the fifth anniversary of the assassination. World War I claimed 8.3 million soldiers and 8 million civilians.

Painting the Sistine Chapel

Michelangelo's vision of God.

HIS ORIGINAL ASSIGNMENT was to paint the dozen apostles around the outside of the chapel's ceiling, but Michelangelo Buonarroti, 33, had a better idea. Why not make the central area of the ceiling his canvas and paint 300 characters from the Old Testament? Lying on his back on scaffolding 65 feet above the floor, he began painting the 44 × 132-foot arched ceiling on May 10, 1508. There was a lot of papal conflict throughout the project. Nevertheless the ceiling was completed October 31, 1512, at which time Michelangelo was paid 3,000 crowns.

The Transcontinental Railroad

The rails are joined at Promontory Point, Utah. Many dignitaries were upset at the historic photograph because of the public display of alcohol.

CALIFORNIA GOVERNOR LELAND STANFORD broke ground for the Central Pacific Railroad at Sacramento, California, January 8, 1863, but the first rails were not spiked to ties until October 26 of that year. While construction snaked eastward through the Sierra Nevada, the Union Pacific broke ground at Omaha, Nebraska, December 2, 1863. Actual work didn't begin there until after the Civil War, July 10, 1865. Finally, on May 10, 1869, the 1,069 miles of Union Pacific track were joined with the 690 miles built by the Central Pacific at Promontory Point, Utah, and America's two coasts were connected by rail.

Skylab

Skylab at work, high above Earth.

THE FIRST AMERICAN SPACE STATION was launched unmanned on May 14, 1973. Technical problems arose a minute into the flight when a meteor shield tore loose. The first crew, Charles Conrad, Paul J. Weitz, and Joseph Kerwin, repaired the problems during their stay from May 25 to June 22, 1973. The fourth and final mission, manned by Gerald Carr, William Pogue, and Edward Gibson, set the record of 84 days. Atmospheric drag caused the orbiting laboratory to fall July 11, 1979. Most of *Skylab* burned when it reentered the atmosphere, although some debris fell in the Indian Ocean and on portions of Australia.

World War II

V-J Day in Times Square, New York City.

ONE-AND-A-HALF-MILLION GERMAN FORCES invaded Poland along a 1,750-mile border controlled by the Third Reich at 4:45 a.m. on September 1, 1939. Chancellor Adolf Hitler issued his statement at 5:11 a.m. Following the attack on Pearl Harbor, the United States and Great Britain declared war on Japan December 8, 1941. Germany declared war on the United States December 11. History's worst war eventually claimed 57 million lives, half of them civilian. The European war ended with the unconditional surrender of Germany signed at Gen. Eisenhower's headquarters in a Reims, France, schoolhouse at 2:41 a.m. May 7, 1945, which went into effect at one minute past midnight on May 9. Emperor Hirohito broadcast Japan's acceptance of unconditional surrender on August 14, 1945; the official document was signed shortly after 8:00 a.m. on September 2 on the battleship *Missouri* in Tokyo Bay.

The Holocaust

A snapshot of a temple going up in flames on Kristallnacht.

THE MASS MURDER OF JEWS by Nazis parallels Germany's war involvement, although their persecution began long before. The Dachau concentration camp opened March 22, 1933, followed a week later by the first in a series of official edicts—a boycott of Jewish shops and businesses. Sanctions crossed over into murder November 9, 1938, with the events of Kristallnacht, "the night of broken glass." Nazi-supported mob violence resulted in 91 murders, 7,500 destroyed businesses, and 267 burned synagogues. Some 25,000 Jewish men were rounded up and sent to concentration camps, beginning a trend that did not stop until the end of World War II. Allied forces liberated Buchenwald on April 10, 1945, Bergen-Belsen on April 15, Dachau on April 29, and finally, Mauthausen on May 5. A total of 5,962,129 Jews, 63 percent of the prewar European population, died in the Holocaust.

Construction of the Erie Canal

A boat on the Mohawk River.

THE FRENCH ENGINEER VAUBAN first suggested a canal to link Lakes Erie and Ontario in 1699. In 1817, Gov. DeWitt Clinton proposed a canal that would connect New York City with the Great Lakes via Albany and Buffalo. Formal construction began at Rome, New York, on July 4, 1817. On October 23, 1819, the 90-mile middle section from Utica to Rome opened. Other sections opened along the way as they were completed. The first official passage from Lake Erie to New York City occurred October 26, 1825. The Erie Canal stretched a distance of 363 miles and was 40 feet wide and four feet deep.

The Revolutionary War

British soldiers kill five Americans at the Boston Massacre, March 5, 1770.

WHAT BEGAN AS A SERIES OF PROTESTS erupted into all-out war between Great Britain and the colonies. Thus, the American Revolution had been going on before actual war broke out at dawn, April 19, 1775, with "the shot heard round the world" at the Battle of Lexington and Concord. American forces engaged 800 British troops. The next major battle was at Bunker Hill the following June 17. For all practical purposes, the war that claimed 4,435 Americans ended with the defeat of Gen. Cornwallis by George Washington's troops at the Battle of Yorktown in 1781. The official end came with the signing of the Treaty of Paris September 3, 1783.

Building the Statue of Liberty

Lady Liberty's head on display in a Parisian park.

EDOUARD LABOULAYE, chairman of the French antislavery society, proposed the idea of a liberty monument for America's centennial in France in 1865. Sculptor Frédéric-Auguste Bartholdi began sketching in 1870. Once his plaster model was approved by the Franco-American Union, Bartholdi's crew began work in November of 1875. There was no way it would be finished by the actual centennial, but the hand and torch were displayed at Philadelphia's Centennial Exposition beginning August 14, 1876. With 120 tons of framework designed by Alexandre-Gustave Eiffel, "Liberty Enlightening the World," was presented to the United States at a ceremony in Paris on July 4, 1884. It was then shipped across the ocean in 241 crates, reassembled, and dedicated on Bedloe's Island October 28, 1886.

10 years, **3** months, **12** days • **1904–13**

Construction of the Panama Canal

Ground-level panorama, 1909.

THE FRENCH BEGAN IT January 1, 1880, but costs and malaria ended their dream in 1889. When negotiations with Colombia failed, the United States recognized the new Republic of Panama, bought rights from the French, and began digging on May 4, 1904. Col. George Goethals supervised the Army Corps of Engineers in moving 240 million cubic yards of earth. Over 70,000 eventually worked on the canal; there were 5,600 deaths during construction, and the total cost was $400 million. The last rock was lifted September 10, 1913. A sailing ship passed through the canal that November, but on August 15, 1914, the USS *Ancon,* piloted by Capt. John A. Constantine, made the first official passage in 9 hours, 40 minutes.

The French Revolution

The execution of King Louis XVI, January 21, 1793.

THE ESTATES GENERAL convened at Versailles to submit their grievances to the crown May 5, 1789. Events escalated with the storming of the Bastille from June 12 to June 14, 1789. Political upheaval transcended into the Reign of Terror (1793–94) beginning with the execution of King Louis XVI on January 21, 1793. The radicals, led by Maximilien Robespierre, gained control of the revolutionary government; Parisian prisons filled. The guillotines averaged 60 beheadings a day. Robespierre himself was executed on July 28, 1794. The twilight of the Revolution coincided with the rise of Napoléon. A new constitution was proclaimed December 15, 1799.

The Longest Administration

Franklin Roosevelt lived in the White House longer than any other president.

FRANKLIN DELANO ROOSEVELT, 51, took the oath of office March 4, 1933. As the country marched out of economic crisis and into a global conflict, Roosevelt was reelected in 1936, 1940, and in the midst of World War II, for an unprecedented fourth term in 1944. Roosevelt died of a massive cerebral hemorrhage at age 63 on April 12, 1945. The elections of 1948 were the first in 20 years that did not have him as a candidate. Due to the passage of the 22nd Amendment in 1951 limiting presidents to two terms, it appears that Roosevelt's record will stand for a long time.

Prohibition

Members of the Women's Organization for National Prohibition Reform
pose for a photograph in 1932.

THE 18TH AMENDMENT to the Constitution was ratified January 16, 1919, and went into effect exactly one year later. President Herbert Hoover called it a "noble experiment," but the move to ban liquor was poorly enforced, and terms like "bathtub gin" and "bootlegger" became part of the national lexicon. Crime empires were built trafficking illegal alcohol. With the onset of the Depression, federal and state legislatures realized that lost tax revenues and unemployed brewers were a problem that could be easily rectified. At 5:32 p.m. on December 5, 1933, Utah became the 36th state to ratify the 21st Amendment, thereby ending national prohibition.

Carving Mount Rushmore

President Franklin Roosevelt was on hand for
the dedication of Thomas Jefferson's head.

SCULPTOR GUTZON BORGLUM planted the American flag atop a granite
slab in South Dakota's Black Hills on October 1, 1925, where he would
carve the heads of his favorite Americans. After a second dedication,
workers began the George Washington carving on October 4, 1927.
President Franklin Roosevelt attended the dedication of the Jefferson
head on August 30, 1936. The Theodore Roosevelt visage was completed
in 1939. Borglum passed away in 1941 before Rushmore was completed—
his son Lincoln supervised the completion. The last day of work was
October 31, 1941.

The Gold Rush

The rush to the diggings produced a handful of millionaires
and many more broken hearts.

JAMES MARSHALL, working at John Sutter's sawmill on California's
American River, discovered gold on January 24, 1848, but the gold rush
didn't start then. The *San Francisco Californian* printed the first gold story
on March 15. By May, it was reported that most able-bodied men had
headed for the diggings. President Polk confirmed the discovery to
Congress on December 5; 30,000 true forty-niners came to California the
following spring. The big year was 1852, with gold production hitting $81
million. Over 300,000 had transplanted themselves by 1854. Ten years after,
in 1864, the rush was over and river and surface placers were exhausted.

15 years, **1** month, **1** day • **1981–96**

The Marriage of Charles and Diana

A commemorative coin from the big event.

PRINCE CHARLES, 32, PRINCE OF WALES, and Lady Diana Spencer, 20, exchanged vows before a worldwide audience at St. Paul's Cathedral in London at the 11:20 a.m. ceremony, July 29, 1981. Their first child, William, was born June 21, 1982. He was followed by Harry on September 15, 1984. Less than two years later, rumors circulated that the royal couple had marital problems. Prime Minister John Major announced to Parliament that the couple was separating in 1992. The divorce became final August 28, 1996. One year and three days later, Diana died in a car crash.

The Reign of the Unabomber

For years, this drawing furnished by the FBI
was the only depiction of the Unabomber.

DUBBED BY THE PRESS because he targeted "un"iversities and "a"irlines,
Theodore Kaczynski, a former assistant mathematics professor at the
University of California, Berkeley, terrorized individuals from a small
cabin near Lincoln, Montana. It began with an unmailed package found
at the University of Illinois, Chicago, May 25, 1978, that exploded and
injured Northwestern campus police officer Terry Marker. RenTech
owner Hugh Scrutton of Sacramento was killed December 11, 1985. In
1994 and 1995, two more fatalities were recorded in New Jersey and one
in Sacramento. After 16 attacks, Kaczynski, 53, was arrested April 16,
1996, on a tip from his brother. He pled guilty in 1998 to actions
resulting in three deaths and 23 injuries.

Cats

The jellical cats came out for many nights while *Cats* ran on Broadway.

BASED ON THE POEMS OF T. S. ELIOT, set to the music of Andrew Lloyd Webber, and populated by characters such as Grizabella and Old Deuteronomy, it was presumed that *Cats* was already a runaway Broadway hit when it opened at the Winter Garden Theatre on October 7, 1982. That it would outlast *A Chorus Line* as history's longest-running musical was something else. When it finally closed September 10, 2000, it had played a total of 7,485 performances in 6,548 days.

Transatlantic Flights of the Concorde

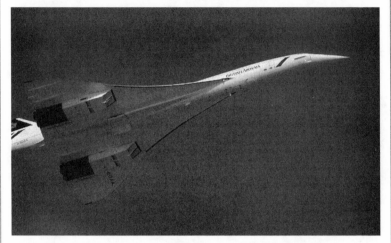

The Concorde in flight. For $10,000 you could go from Paris to Boston
in a little over three hours.

THE FIRST CONCORDE, the supersonic passenger jet designed to cross the
Atlantic in three hours at altitudes of 60,000 feet and speeds of 1,370
mph, was test-flown on March 2, 1969, in the skies over France. The first
London–New York commercial flight occurred on November 22, 1977.
The first Concorde to fly around the world, 28,238 miles, did so in 1986
in 29 hours, 59 minutes. A crash in Paris in July 2000 claimed 113 lives
and signaled the beginning of the end for the unique airplanes. The last,
celebrity-laden transatlantic flight touched down at London's Heathrow
Airport just after 4:00 p.m. on October 24, 2003.

Nelson Mandela's Imprisonment

A freed Mandela pays a visit to his cell on Robben Island in 1994.

MANDELA WAS SENTENCED to five years in prison in 1962 for illegally leaving the country and inciting workers to riot. While incarcerated, he was convicted of treason and sabotage in 1964 and sentenced to life in prison. He spent 18 years in the maximum-security prison on Robben Island, off the coast of South Africa. His mother died in 1968, and his eldest son was killed in a car accident in 1969. He was denied permission to attend either funeral. International pressure for his release increased in the 1980s; it is believed that embargoes cost his country $4 billion between 1988 and 1990. Mandela was finally released on February 11, 1990. He received the Nobel Peace Prize in 1993, and the following year he was elected president of South Africa.

The Berlin Wall

President Ronald Reagan delivers his famous address at the Berlin Wall.

THE BARRIER between East and West Berlin was closed shortly after midnight on August 13, 1961, leaving one-half of the city under the East German Communist regime and the other half free. Over time, four generations of walls reinforced the 27-mile blockade. The most visible symbol of the Cold War was threatened by new policies of Mikhail Gorbachev in the 1980s, and a challenge in 1987 from President Reagan to "tear down this wall." On November 9, 1989, the East German government announced the opening of the border, and the wall came tumbling down. Over the years, 192 people lost their lives trying to escape to freedom.

The Twin Towers of the World Trade Center

As this shot from the early 1980s attests, the Towers dominated the New York City skyline.

ARCHITECT MINORU YAMASAKI unveiled his design in January 1964. Groundbreaking ceremonies were held August 5, 1966, and production commenced, supervised by Emery Roth and Sons. One World Trade Center opened in December 1970. Ribbon cutting for Two World Trade Center came April 4, 1973. The structures contained 200,000 tons of steel, 425,000 cubic yards of concrete, and had 43,600 windows. Each tower weighed 500,000 tons. A total of 10,000 workers were involved in the construction that took seven years, seven months, 30 days. Both towers were demolished when terrorists crashed hijacked airliners into them September 11, 2001.

American Involvement in the Vietnam War

Thunderchief pilots, flying under radar control with a B-66 destroyer, bomb a military target over North Vietnam, June 14, 1966.

LT. COL. A. PETER DEWEY, the first American killed in Vietnam, was head of the OSS mission and mistaken for a Frenchman on September 26, 1945. Following a century of colonial rule, the French were forced out in July 1954. The U.S.-backed Republic of Vietnam formed in 1955. After attacks on two American ships, full-fledged military involvement resulted in the 1964 Gulf of Tonkin Resolution. A cease-fire, signed in Paris January 27, 1973, resulted in the departure of the last U.S.-combat soldiers. On April 30, 1975, two U.S. Marines killed in a rocket attack at Saigon's Tan Son Nhut airport became the last Americans to die in combat. Later that day North Vietnamese tanks rolled into Saigon, and the war was over. America's most unpopular war cost over $150 billion and more than 58,000 lives.

The Thirty Years' War

The castle at Ehrenbreitenstein at the junction of the Rhein and Moselle Rivers, a strategic focal point of the Thirty Years' War.

IT BEGAN WITH BOHEMIAN REVOLTS against the Holy Roman Empire, but eventually involved many European nations, particularly Germany. Northern Germany supported Protestants; southern Germany, Austria, and Spain supported Catholics. Sweden and France wanted to destroy the Austrian Hapsburgs. The Peace of Westphalia in 1648 upheld the survival of the German Protestant states, recognized independence for Switzerland and the Netherlands, and increased the status of Sweden, Prussia, and France.

The War of the Roses

The Battle of Bosworth, August 22, 1485, where Richard III was defeated and slain.
According to Shakespeare, this is where Richard said, "My kingdom for a horse."

THE ROOTS OF ENGLAND'S CONFLICT began in 1399, when Henry IV of the red-rosed house of Lancaster took power from Richard II. Their enemies, the Yorks, wore badges of white roses. It was an uneasy time. Both houses were descended from King Edward III; however, there was some madness on the part of King Henry VI and much civil unrest. The opening battle, a York victory, was the first battle of Saint Albans on May 22, 1455. The last major conflict, Bosworth, saw the defeat of Richard III by Henry Tudor, aka Henry VI, ushering in the rule of the Tudors. The Yorks mounted a last gasp at the Battle of Stoke, June 16, 1487, but were defeated by Henry VII.

The Imprisonment of Rudolf Hess

Exactly why Hess made his mystery flight is still unclear.

HITLER'S "DEPUTY OF THE FÜHRER," his secretary, and the editor of *Mein Kampf,* Hess parachuted from a Messerschmitt BF110 into Scotland May 10, 1941, saying he was there to negotiate peace. Hitler knew nothing about it. The English imprisoned Hess in the Tower of London and considerd him mentally unstable. Facts revealed after the war, however, show that he might have been lured by some strange plot hatched by none other than James Bond creator Ian Fleming. Hess was given a life sentence at Nuremberg. He hanged himself at age 93 at the Spandau War Crimes Prison, August 17, 1987.

The Reign of Queen Victoria

An early picture of the queen and her true love, Prince Albert.

VICTORIA WAS 18 when she ascended to the throne June 20, 1837, following the death of her uncle William IV. Her reign, the longest in British history, was the backdrop to an era that included the first opium war, the Crimean, Zulu, and Boer Wars, the literary careers of Charles Dickens and H. G. Wells, the development of the railroad, the discovery of gold in Africa, and the imperial rule of India. Victoria was queen of the United Kingdom of Great Britain and Ireland until her death on the Isle of Wight January 22, 1901.

The Soviet Union

The great Socialist Revolution Parade in Moscow, November 7, 1983.

FOLLOWING RUSSIA'S OCTOBER REVOLUTION which ousted the czar, and the civil war between the Bolsheviks and anti-Bolsheviks that raged from 1918 to 1920, the Union of Soviet Socialist Republics was formed December 30, 1922, the first state to be based on Marxist socialism. Bolshevik Vladimir Lenin was the first leader. In 1924, Joseph Stalin emerged as Lenin's successor and ruled with an iron fist until his death in 1953. In the 1980s, a period of "glasnost," or openness, a practice that led to upheavals on several levels, prevailed. The USSR was ultimately dissolved on December 31, 1991.

How Long the *Titanic* Was Lost

Today the *Titanic* rests in an underwater version of a sloping alpine meadow, where the water pressure is 6,000 pounds per square inch.

THE GREAT LUXURY SHIP RMS *Titanic* sank the morning of April 15, 1912, and broke in half. The two pieces rested at a depth of 12,640 feet a thousand miles due east of Boston and 375 miles southeast of St. John's, Newfoundland. They were discovered September 1, 1985, by a group using modern underwater technology led by Dr. Robert D. Ballard. Since the discovery, some 6,000 artifacts have been successfully recovered.

The Orbit of Halley's Comet

Mark Twain predicted his own death with Halley's Comet, figuring that he "came in"
with it in 1835, and that he was bound to "go out" with it in 1910.
Twain died April 21, 1910.

ASTRONOMER EDMOND HALLEY correctly predicted that a comet that had
been seen in 1531, 1607, and 1682 would return in 1758. He didn't live
to see it, but the scientific community was so impressed by this feat of
astronomy and mathematics that they named it after him. The gravitational pull of planets has varied the orbits—it returned in 79.3 years in
1066 when it was seen at the Battle of Hastings (and commemorated in
the Bayeaux Tapestry), and 76.0 years on its last appearance in 1986.
Halley's Comet returns in 2061.

The Lifespan of the Queen Mother

The Queen Mother, commemorated on a British stamp.

BORN A COMMONER August 4, 1900, Elizabeth Angela-Marguerite Bowes-Lyon, Lady Elizabeth was the daughter of Lord Glamis, the 14th Earl of Strathmore and Kinghorne. She married the second son of the king and queen, HRH the Duke of York, on April 26, 1923. Their first child, Princess Elizabeth, was born in 1926. The grand old duke ascended to the throne as King George VI when Edward VIII abdicated in 1936, and his wife became the Queen Consort. A source of strength in World War II, she was in Buckingham Palace when it was bombed in 1940. She became the Queen Mother in 1952 upon the death of her husband and the coronation of her daughter. She remained a public fixture throughout the rest of her life. Elizabeth was honored on her 90th birthday in 1990, attending 118 events. She died in her sleep March 30, 2002.

The Hundred Years' War

Henry V defeats the French in the mud at the
Battle of Agincourt, October 25, 1415.

THIS LONG-RUNNING SERIES OF CONFLICTS that included raids, sieges, naval
battles, and a few uneasy peaces between England and France began
May 24, 1337. French King Philip VI tried to confiscate British territory
in Aquitaine in southern France. The English won many of the battles of
the first part of the war including Crécy, Poitiers, and Agincourt. With
the siege of Orléans in 1429, the tide turned for the French thanks to a
savvy teen warrior, Joan of Arc. For the next quarter century, the French
were victorious. The final battle, Castillon, came July 14, 1453, when
Henry VI tried one last time to gain some French territory for the
crown. The attack was repulsed. The English were expelled from France
for good.

How Long Mount St. Helens Went Between Eruptions

St. Helens erupts on May 18, 1980, for the first time since before the Civil War.

MOUNT ST. HELENS, located 50 miles northeast of Portland, Oregon, in Washington State, is a young volcano, right around 40,000 years old. Dormant since 1857, it smoldered for months before erupting at 8:32 a.m. May 18, 1980, following a 5.1 earthquake a mile beneath its surface. A 2,200-year-old cone collapsed, at least 65 people died, and 150 square miles were destroyed. The 1,300-degree lava was 120 feet deep in some places. The cleanup cost over a billion dollars. The 1980 eruption, as strong as it was, couldn't match the one of 1480, believed to have been five times stronger.

The Aztec Empire

An Aztec artist depicting the subjugation
of the Spaniards.

THE ANCIENT AZTECS completed what is believed to be a 200-year
southern migration from northern Mexico into the Valley of Mexico
around 1193. In 1325 they began to build the city of Tenochtitlán on two
islands in Lake Texcoco on the site of present-day Mexico City. Emperor
Montezuma II was filled with a sense of foreboding a decade before the
Spanish conquistadors arrived, led by Hernán Cortés on November 8,
1519. Montezuma was quickly taken into captivity, and died mysteriously
the day the Aztecs drove the Spaniards away, July 10, 1520. Cortés returned
with more soldiers and Indian allies May 31, 1521, and launched a 75-day
siege. Victory for the conquistadors came August 13, 1521, and the Aztec
empire was no more.

The Qing Dynasty

Qing Ren Zong (Jia Qing) reigned from 1796 to 1821, during which time he became the King of Vietnam and banned Christian literature from China. He was known for his generosity and benevolence.

THE MANCHUS were descendants of the Jin, 12th-century rulers of northern China. They began their dynasty by making the war leader Nurhachi's six-year-old grandson, Shunzhi, the emperor. Among the changes noted by Western culture, the Qings made Chinese men shave their heads and wear long braids known as queues. A long period of peace saw this dynasty heavily involved in international trade. After 2,000 years, the imperial system, which had reached its zenith with the Qings, collapsed with the 1911 revolution. The last emperor, Puyi, was six at the time.

The Renaissance

Botticelli produced *The Birth of Venus* around 1485.

ALTHOUGH HISTORIANS OF THE 19TH CENTURY first used the term, from the French word for *rebirth,* the true timing of the Renaissance depended on what country you were in. In Germany the years were roughly from 1490 to 1600 and in England from 1500 to 1600, but scholars usually agree that it began in Italy with the birth of Petrarch in 1304 and ended with the death of Titian in 1576. Earmarks of the era included a revival of learning, a revival of antiquity, a new appreciation of arts and litera-ture, and new horizons for philosophy and science. Social and economic reform also flourished during the Renaissance.

The Ming Dynasty

From the Ming Dynasty, *Lofty Scholars in a Ravine,* a painting by Wen Cheng.

AFTER A CENTURY OF MONGOLIAN RULE, the Ming dynasty restored tradition beginning with the reign of Hongwu (1368–98). "Ming" means brilliant, and for this dynasty it meant a return to the customs and traditions that had disappeared during the reign of the Mongol tribes. In 1406, construction began on the Forbidden City of Beijing, which was used continuously for 500 years. The last Ming emperor was Chongzhen (1628–44), who hanged himself from a locust tree when his city was overrun by Manchu forces.

African Slavery in the Americas

Of human bondage: a slave sale in Easton, Maryland.
Inset: a handbill for a slave sale.

IMPORTING CAPTURED AFRICANS to work in bondage in the New World began January 22, 1510, when King Ferdinand of Spain authorized 50 slaves to be shipped to Santo Domingo. On August 18, 1518, Charles V granted permission to bring 4,000 more slaves to New Spain. Dutch traders brought slaves to Jamestown, Virginia, in August 1619. By the time of the American Revolution there were perhaps 300,000 slaves. In 1790, 697,624 African slaves were listed in the first U.S. Census. By 1830, the number had jumped to 2,009,043, and in 1860 it was 3,993,760. President Lincoln signed the Emancipation Proclamation in 1862, but it wasn't until December 6, 1865, when the 13th Amendment was ratified, that the practice of slavery was officially abolished in the United States. (Technically, slavery continued in the region for another 20 years—Cuba formally abolished the practice on October 7, 1886.

The Spanish Inquisition

The Court of Inquisition Chaired by St. Dominic by Pedro Berruguette.
The Inquisition itself earned its reputation in the first 15 years of
existence, when 2,000 people were burned as heretics.

POPE SIXTUS IV AUTHORIZED THE SPANISH INQUISITION in 1478, a time
when Catholicism was believed to be in jeopardy by pseudoconverts
from Judaism (Marranos) and Islam (Moriscos). The Grand Inquisitor,
Tomás de Torquemada, of Jewish descent, nevertheless convinced Spanish
authorities to expel all Jews from Spain in 1492 and was responsible for
at least 2,000 executions. A brief respite occurred after Galileo Galilei
was tried and convicted in 1633. However, Ferdinand VII began the tri-
bunals again in 1814. The Spanish Inquisition was officially suppressed
by decree on July 15, 1834.

The Ottoman Empire

Coin of the kingdom from the mid-1700s, a silver
piastre from the Ottoman Empire.

THE OTTOMAN DYNASTY began in the 13th century under King Osman
Al Ghazi. Sultan Suleiman I ("The Magnificent") was the most famous
figure of the era; his reign is regarded as the period of greatest justice and
harmony in any Islamic state. At one point in the 16th century, the empire
reached from the Polish border to the Persian Gulf and from Algeria to the
Caspian Sea—occupying much of present-day Israel, Iraq, Lebanon, Syria,
and Yemen—as well as sections of the Balkans and Caucasus Mountains.
Decline began under Suleiman's son, Selim II. The breakup began with
the secularization of Turkey at the end of World War I.

The Mongol Empire

A 14th-century artist depicts a day in the life of Genghis Khan.

THE NOMADIC TRIBES of the Steppes were united in 1206 by Emperor Temujin, who took the name Genghis Khan. He and his sons created an empire that reached as far west as Iraq and Russia and as far south as India. Genghis Khan invaded China in 1211 and India in 1221. His son Ogadei ("The Great Khan") attacked Russia, Hungary, and Poland over a three-year period ending in 1241. Persia was invaded from 1251 to 1265, and Baghdad was sacked in 1258. Kubla Khan took over in 1259 and created China's Yuan dynasty. The empire of Tamerlane flourished at Samarkand from 1369 to 1405. The Mongol Empire did not disappear overnight, but was absorbed in Russia and fragmented elsewhere. Mongolia was eventually brought under Chinese rule in 1696.

The Roman Empire

The Roman Empire around 395.

THE EMPIRE OF ANCIENT ROME was established January 17, 27 B.C., when Octavius received the title Augustus Caesar from the Senate. He had maneuvered his political career since the assassination of his great-uncle, Julius Caesar, in 44 B.C. After receiving his name change, he ruled for another 44 years. The split into Eastern and Western Roman Empires came in A.D. 395 during the reign of Theodosius the Great. The Eastern Empire became the Byzantine Empire and went on for another millennium. The fall of the Roman Empire came when the Western Empire ended in A.D. 476 with the Goths dethroning Emperor Romulus Augustulus.

The Classic Mayan Era

The Mayans were fascinated by the passage of time, although
their ways of calculating it were hardly digital.

THERE WAS A "PRECLASSIC" Mayan era, beginning around 2600 B.C., when
language developed and towns were constructed. Beginning around A.D.
250, one of the great pre-Columbian civilizations of the ancient Americas
flourished on the Yucatán peninsula and in Guatemala, complete with
stone palaces and temples. Early independent city-states included Copán
and Palenque; later cities in the northern Yucatán were Chichen Itzá,
Uxmal, and Mayapán. Mayan society developed around strong beliefs in
their calendar, astronomy, and mathematics. Possible climate changes and
food shortages around 850 contributed to their demise. Spanish conquest
was completed in 1697 with the fall of Tayasal.

The Middle Ages

In a 15th-century miniature, peasants harvest while the feudal lord lives well.

THERE WAS NO STARTING GUN for the Middle Ages, and the dates vary with every nation, but the era roughly stretches from the fall of the Roman Empire to the fall of Constantinople. In addition to kings, queens, and feudal lords, a lot of power was wielded by the Roman Catholic Church. From the start-up until around the 12th century was a time known as the Dark Ages, when the cultures of the early Greeks and Romans were largely and officially ignored. Other major events of the Middle Ages included the rise of the Holy Roman Empire, the Black Death, and the Hundred Years' War.

The Holy Roman Empire

Charlemagne and His Scholars by Karl von Blaas. "The greatest of the medieval kings," according to Will Durant, lived from 742 to 814, dying in the 47th year of his reign.

IT BEGAN WHEN Pope Leo III crowned Charlemagne as emperor on Christmas Day, 800, and eventually became the mightiest political force in Europe. The empire consisted of German states and princedoms, and since the emperors were elected, almost every royal German house ruled at one time or another. Frederick II's reign was highlighted by the Fifth Crusade (1228–29) that took Jerusalem from the Turks. The most influential leaders were Maximilian I (1486–1519) and Charles V (1519–58). Power declined when the latter gave up the crown in 1556. In 1806 Napoléon forced Francis II to abandon the title of emperor, reorganized the German states, and officially abolished the Holy Roman Empire.

The Byzantine Empire

From the 19th-century costume book by
Munich's Braun and Schneider circa 1861, a
servant, a Byzantine empress, and a princess.

THE GREEK DIVISION of the Roman Empire, the Eastern Roman Empire
was a civilization centered at the capital city at Byzantium established
by the Roman emperor, Constantine the Great. He renamed his city
Constantinople, which is present-day Istanbul. While the empire in the
west declined and eventually fell in 476, the one in the east flourished. It
ended in 1453 when Constantinople was captured by Ottoman Turkish
forces under Sultan Muhammad II.

Early Greek Civilization

Greek athletes are celebrated on this vase
from around 500 B.C.

SHORTLY AFTER THE "DARK AGES OF GREECE" ended came the evolution
of mythology and an alphabet. The first Olympics were held in 776 B.C.
Homer wrote the *Iliad* and the *Odyssey* between 750 and 700 B.C. The
First Messenian War took place around 730 B.C. The city-states of Sparta
and Athens went to war again in the Second Peloponnesian War (431–
405 B.C.). Socrates was executed in 399 B.C.; Plato opened the Academy
in 386 B.C. Two years later Aristotle was born. The Macedonian general
Alexander the Great built the capital at Alexandria in 332 B.C. The
decline came when the Roman general Sulla conquered Athens in
86 B.C. Then the Goths overran Athens along with Sparta and Corinth
in 267 A.D., and finally, Emperor Diocletian divided the Roman Empire
in two, re-forming modern Greece as the Byzantine Empire in 286 A.D.

2,267 years • **7th century B.C.–1568**

Construction of the Great Wall of China

Tourists flock to the Great Wall.

THE WARRING STATES began by constructing various sections of the "10,000-li Great Wall" as early at the seventh century B.C. In 214 B.C., Gen. Meng Jian received orders from Qin Shi Huangdi to join sections of the earlier wall to form a blockade for the empire's northern and western borders. The wall was of varying heights, as low as 23 feet and as high at 46 feet. Workers toiled in deserts and mountains; many were buried within the wall itself. Renovations depended on the times—the Ming Dynasty began one in 1368 that lasted 200 years. The Great Wall stretches 1,674 miles east to west from Shanhaiguan in Shandong to Jiayuguan in Gansu.

The Reign of the Pharoahs

King Tutankhamen's mask, discovered by Howard
Carter in the Valley of the Kings in 1922.

THE HEYDAY OF ANCIENT EGYPT is distinguished by 31 dynasties, along
with brief periods of occupation. The first through third dynasties
(2950 B.C.– 2575 B.C.) created the capital of Memphis near present Cairo
and started building pyramids. The Old Kingdom, the fourth through
eighth dynasties (2575 B.C.–2150 B.C.), produced the Great Pyramids at
Giza and Dahshur. The New Kingdom (18th–20th Dynasties, 1539 B.C.–
1075 B.C.) included the short tenure of King Tutankhamen, and the
67-year reign of Rameses II. The Greco-Roman period, from 332 B.C.
to A.D. 395, saw the occupation of Alexander the Great, the dynasty
started by Alexander's general Ptolemy, the carving of the Rosetta stone
(196 B.C.), and the reign of Cleopatra VII (51–30 B.C.). In 30 B.C., Egypt
became a province of the Roman Empire.

The Julian Period

Joseph Scaliger, from an engraving by J. de Leeuw. "I was born at Agen, in Guienne, in the year 1540, on the fourth of August, fourteen hours after noon: so that my birthday is reckoned the fifth of August, civil time."

IN 1582, French classical scholar Joseph Scaliger created the Julian period in an effort to assign positive numbers to dates, rather than have to deal with B.C. and A.D. He named his method after his father, Julius Caesar Scaliger (1484–1558). According to Scaliger, the Julian day one began at noon, January 1, 4713 B.C., because it was the most recent time that three cycles had begun on the same day—the 28-year solar cycle, the 19-year lunar cycle, and the 15-year indiction cycle, used to regulate taxes in ancient Rome. It will take 7,980 years to complete the period, the product of 28, 19, and 15. Astronomers use the system to assign a unique number to every day since January 1, 4713 B.C. The Julian period will conclude in 3267, a mere 7,980 years after its origination.

Comet Kohoutek's Orbit

The comet Kohoutek, photographed by *Skylab* on December 21, 1973.

WHAT WAS SUPPOSED TO BE *the* celestial event from 1973 to 1974 turned out to be a bit of a dud. Lubos Kohoutek of the Hamburg Observatory discovered Comet Kohoutek (1973 XII) on March 7, 1973, while he was looking for asteroid images on photographic plates. It came closest to the sun December 28, 1973, but was best viewed from Earth on January 15, 1974. *Skylab* got some great photographs, but for most terrestrials, the view was hardly spectacular. Hopefully, we'll have better luck next time.

The Last Ice Age

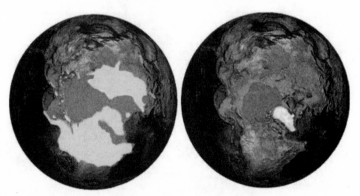

The last glacial advance of the Pleistocene epoch. On the left, a good portion of North America is covered by ice as heavy as two miles thick. (Glacial ice is white, sea ice is dark gray.) On the right, where the ice is today.

MORE THAN 20 GLACIAL ADVANCES and retreats have occurred over the past 2 million years or so. Before that, major glaciations occurred between 800 and 600 million years ago, then again between about 350 and 250 million years ago, and finally during the last 4 million years. Less extensive glaciations, but chilly temperatures nevertheless, occurred between 460 and 430 million years ago. The last one, which began approximately 85,000 years ago, buried North America and Europe under about two miles of ice. It peaked about 18,000 years ago, covering Britain as far south as Wales while glaciers created Long Island. Although the ice receded about 10,000 years ago, the period itself ended only 7,000 years ago.

The Oldest Humans

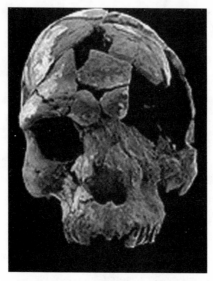

The oldest skull caused quite a stir when it
was unearthed in Ethiopia in 1997.

DISCOVERED IN THE MIDDLE AWASH AREA of central Ethiopia in 1997,
the skulls of two adults and a child were carbon-dated and found to be
154,000 and 160,000 years old—some 50,000 years older than the previous oldest Homo sapiens, or modern human, discoveries. The skulls
were found near a village called Herto in the Afar region. It was a major
breakthrough in anthropology, suggesting that we might have descended
not from the European Neanderthals, but from humans living in Africa.

The Cenozoic Era

Arizona's recent Barringer Crater, at 30,000 years old, was not formed by the meteor that may have taken the dinosaurs.

THIS HAS BEEN A LONG ERA, and we are still in it. From the Greek word meaning "new life," it began 65 million years ago—when the meteor that allegedly took the dinosaurs smashed into the earth. The Cenozoic era is divided into two periods, the Quaternary and the Tertiary. Mammals spread out and diversified, as did birds, flowers, insects, and bony fish. Then, the first humans appeared in the last two million years.

The Mesozoic Era

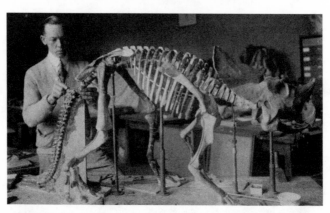

In 1921, Norman Ross of the division of paleontology at the National Museum reconstructs the skeleton of a baby triceratops found in Montana.

KNOWN AS THE "Age of Medieval Life," the Mesozoic era lasted from 248 million to 65 million years ago. It consisted of the Triassic period (248 to 213 million years ago) that saw the breakup of the continent Pangea, the Jurassic period (213 to 145 million years ago) with giant herbivorous dinosaurs like the brachiosaurus and diplodocus noshing on ferns and palmy *cycads,* and finally the "Age of Dinosaurs," the Cretaceous period (145 to 65 million years ago). During that last era of the dinosaurs, insects, the first mammals, and many flower groups appeared. Dinosaurs ruled for some 180 million years, but disappeared right after a meteor struck the earth, leading many to believe that some drastic environmental change was the reason.

The Oldest Living Thing

Miners at the Waste Isolation Pilot Plant use a Marietta Drum Miner
to cut passages and rooms 2,150 feet underground in
ancient stable salt deposits.

IN THE YEAR 2000, ancient bacteria—microbes trapped in suspended animation—were found in salt crystals buried 2,000 feet below a cavern in southeast New Mexico. Found while drilling an air intake shaft in the world's first radioactive waste dump, the bacterium *Bacillus* strain 2-9-3 resembles strains previously found in the Dead Sea.

The Paleozoic Era

A 455-million-year-old trilobite fossil.

DIVIDED INTO SEVEN PERIODS (Cambrian, Ordovician, Silurian, Devonian, Mississippian, Pennsylvanian, and Permian), the Paleozoic era ("Age of Ancient Life") dates from 570 million to 248 million years ago. It came just after the Precambrian and just before the Mesozoic eras, and is marked by two major events. Multicelled animals had an explosion in diversity, making most living animal forms appear in a relatively short period of time, a few million years. The other is a mass extinction that claimed about 90 percent of all marine life.

The Oldest Insect Fossil

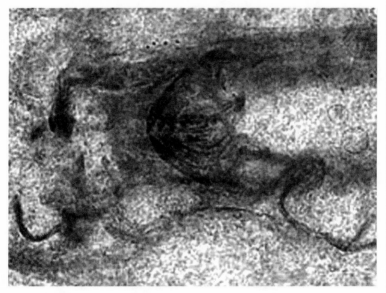

A pair of jaws are all that remain of the world's oldest insect fossil.

THIS FOSSIL REMAINED IN A DRAWER for a century at the Natural History Museum in London. Scientists now believe a set of minuscule jaws pushes the appearance of insects on Earth back some 10 to 20 million years. They also believe this creature flew, which moves the first flight back to a time 70 million years before the oldest fossilized insect wing. This all means insects were buzzing about 170 million years before dinosaurs first appeared.

The Precambrian Eon

A satellite image of the Precambrian greenstone belt
at Burkina Faso, West Africa.

SCIENTISTS DESIGNATE THIS ERA as the amount of time that passed from
the formation of the earth until the first complex life-forms appeared.
The crust cooled, the moon formed, and an atmosphere developed that
slowly became oxygen enriched. Fossilized algae from this era, 3 billion
years old, have been found in South African rocks. The oldest of the
geologic eras accounts for about 80 percent of the earth's time.

4.6 billion years

The Earth

Africa and Saudi Arabia are visible in this view from *Apollo XVII.*
Probably the most-requested picture of Earth, it was taken by
astronauts as they left Earth's orbit en route to the moon. Taken
on December 7, 1972, it was the first time that the trajectory of
an Apollo mission enabled a view of the South Pole.

ALMOST ALL THE EVENTS DESCRIBED HEREIN happened on Earth, or in the
space above it, or on its only moon. Trying to comprehend this amount
of time is not an easy task. In his book *Basin and Range,* John McPhee
painted a good picture. Hold your arms out to each side and imagine
the time of Earth's history as the distance from the tips of your fingers
on your left hand to the tips of the fingers on your right. Now, look at
your middle finger on your right hand. From the bottom to the top of
the nail, that's how long humans have been here.

13.7 to **14.5** billion years

The Universe

The Advanced Camera for Surveys (ACS) recently installed aboard the Hubble
Telescope records this image of the Cone Nebula, about 2,700 light years away.
NASA describes it as "a craggy-looking mountaintop of cold gas and dust,"
and a "celestial maternity ward . . . where stars and perhaps
embryonic planetary systems are forming."

OF ALL THE TIMES IN THIS BOOK, this is the one most likely to change.
Not only is the universe expanding, our perception of its age changes all
the time. In 1995, the estimate was from 8 to 12 billion years, but there
were known stars in our own galaxy older than that. Before that, scientists put the number at somewhere between 10 and 20 billion years.
Astronomer Edwin Hubble first noticed that galaxies were rushing away
from each other at a rate proportional to their distance. Using the telescope that bears his name, scientists are closing in on a more precise time
that dates from the Big Bang to today. As of this writing, NASA is
preparing to launch an even more powerful telescope designed to
unlock more of the amazing secrets of space and time.

Index of Events

Photo Credits

Arizona Historical Society, 7

Author Collection, 3

Chicago Historical Society, 9

Clemson University Strom Thurmond Collection, 42

Gary Taustine, Manhattan, 28

International News Service, 123

Library of Congress, 4, 14, 25, 26, 30, 35, 37, 40, 43, 45, 48, 49, 50, 52, 53, 57, 61, 63, 65, 68, 69, 71, 72, 75, 76, 78, 80, 81, 82, 84, 89, 91, 94, 96, 106, 110, 116, 117, 121, 122, 124, 143, 164, 166

Los Angeles Times, 92

Martha Swope, 127

Max Frankel, 115

National Aeronautics and Space Administration (NASA), 13, 20, 23, 31, 34, 41, 56, 87, 113, 139, 160, 161, 163, 168, 169, 170

National Archives and Records Administration, 1, 2, 5, 6, 8, 10, 12, 15, 16, 17, 18, 19, 21, 22, 24, 27, 29, 32, 33, 36, 38, 39, 44, 46, 47, 51, 54, 55, 58, 59, 60, 62, 64, 66, 67, 70, 73, 74, 77, 79, 83, 85, 86, 88, 90, 95, 97, 98, 100, 101, 102, 103, 104, 107, 108, 109, 111, 114, 118, 119, 120, 125, 126, 129, 130, 131, 132, 133, 134, 135, 136, 137, 138, 140, 141, 144, 145, 146, 147, 148, 149, 150, 152, 153, 154, 155, 156, 157, 158, 159, 162, 165, 167

New York Daily News, 93

Plane and Pilot, 128

Time Life Pictures/Getty Images, 66, 99

U.S. Army, 105

U.S. Army Corps of Engineers, 142

Union Pacific Railroad Museum, 112

University of Texas at Austin, 151

U.S. Drug Enforcement Administration, 11